ICE CREAM COLORING BOOK FOR ADULTS

CRYSTAL
COLORING BOOKS

ISBN: 9781090743008

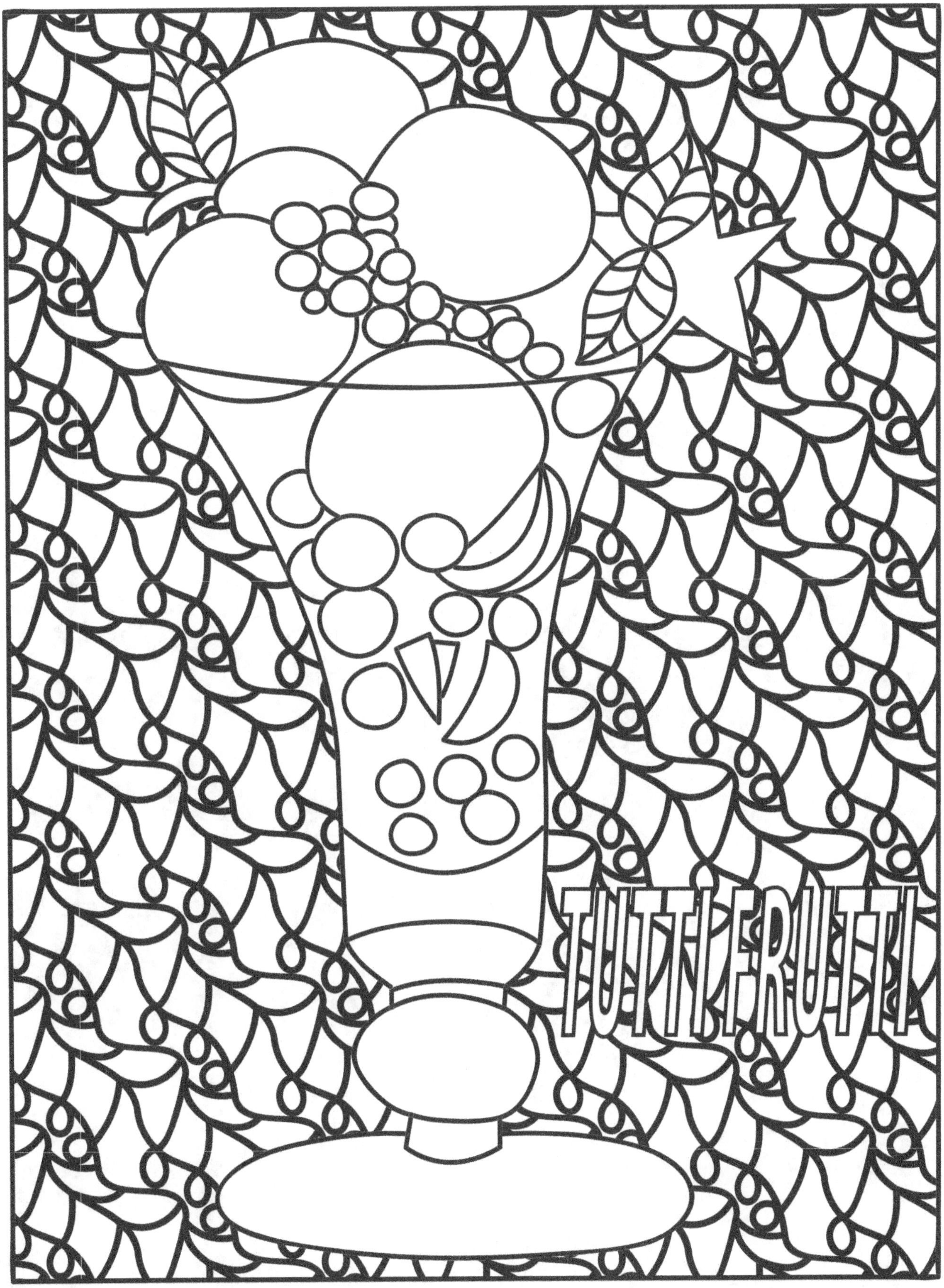
TUTTI FRUTTI

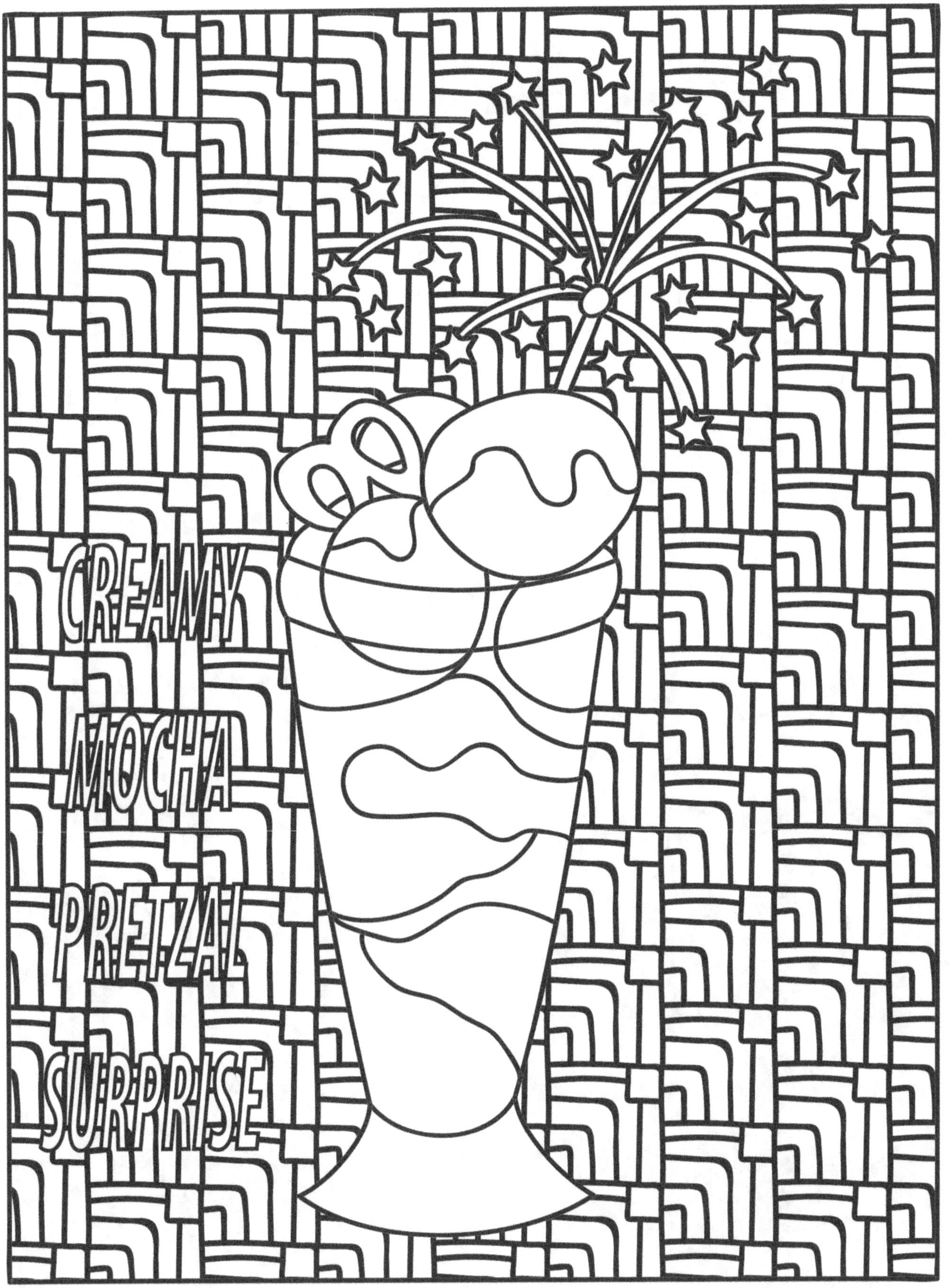
CREAMY
MOCHA
PRETZAL
SURPRISE

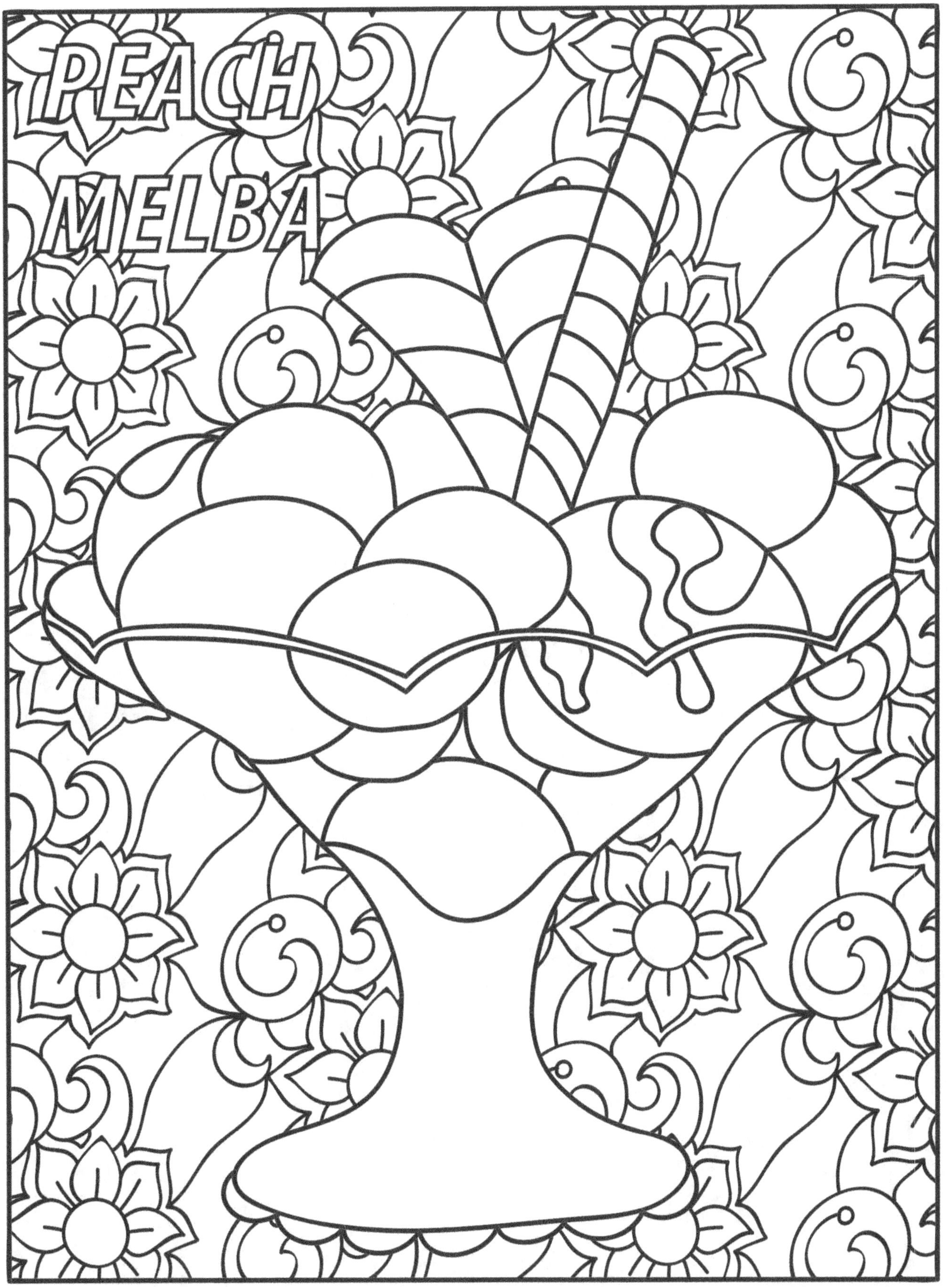
PEACH
MELBA

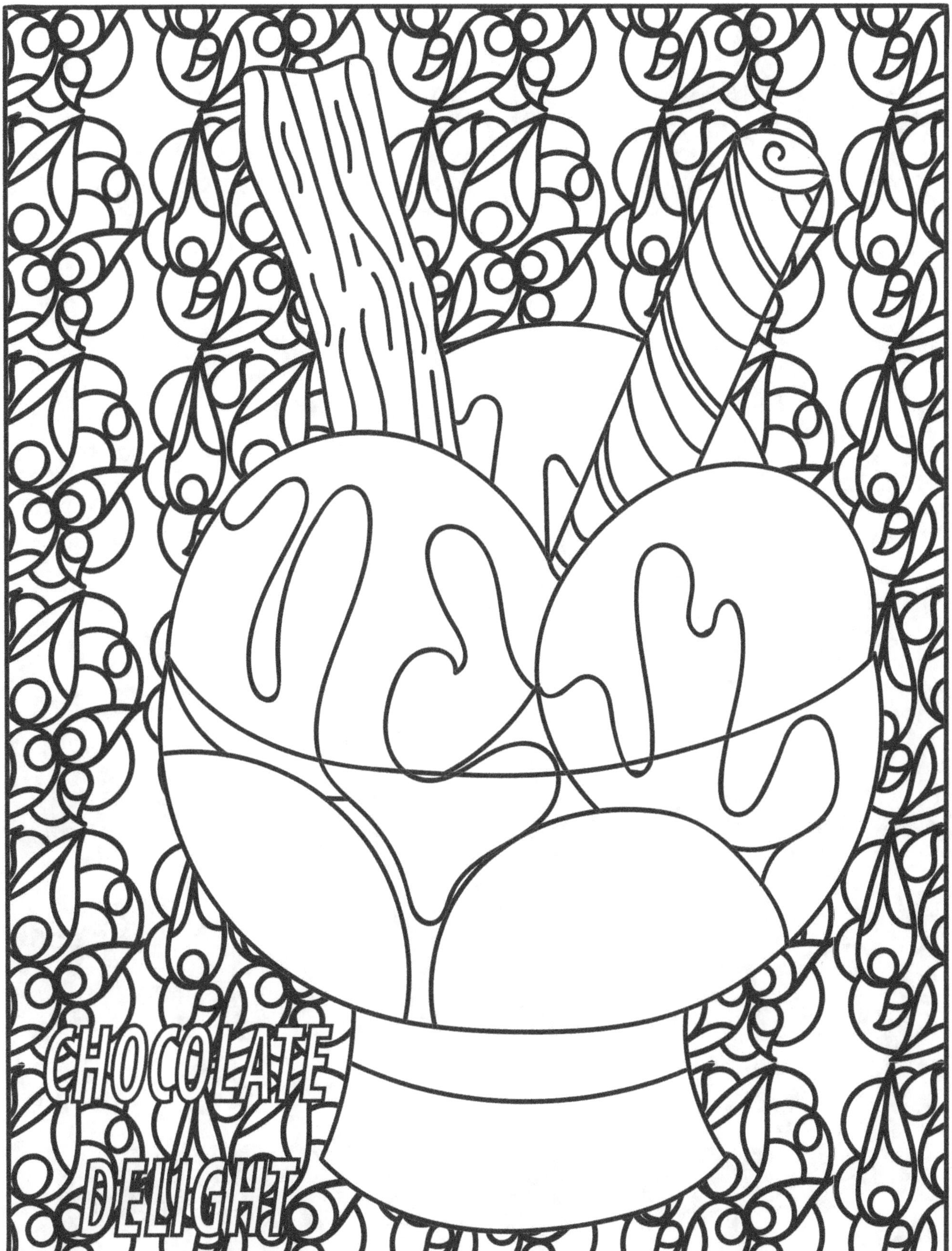
CHOCOLATE
DELIGHT

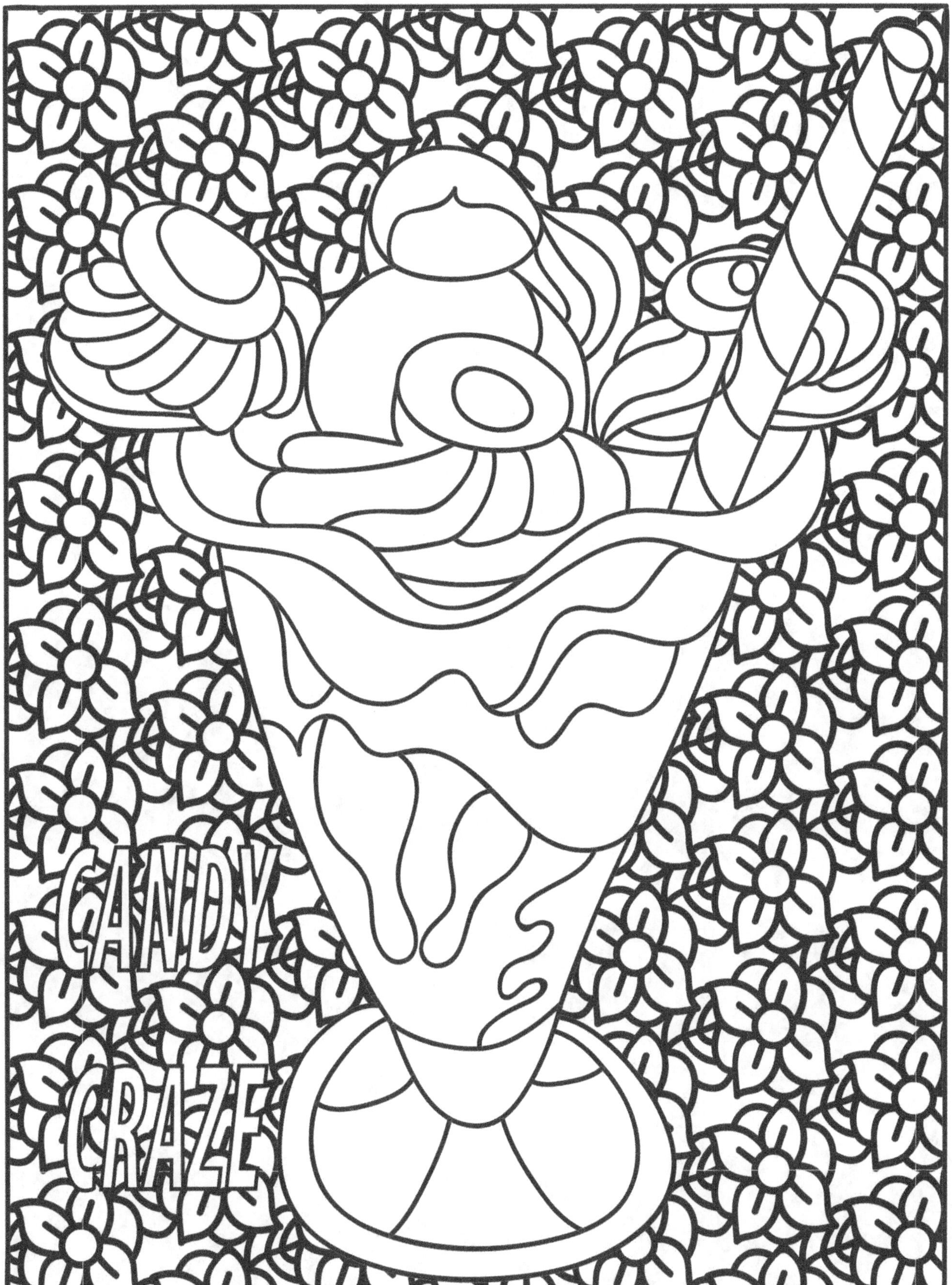
CANDY
CRAZE

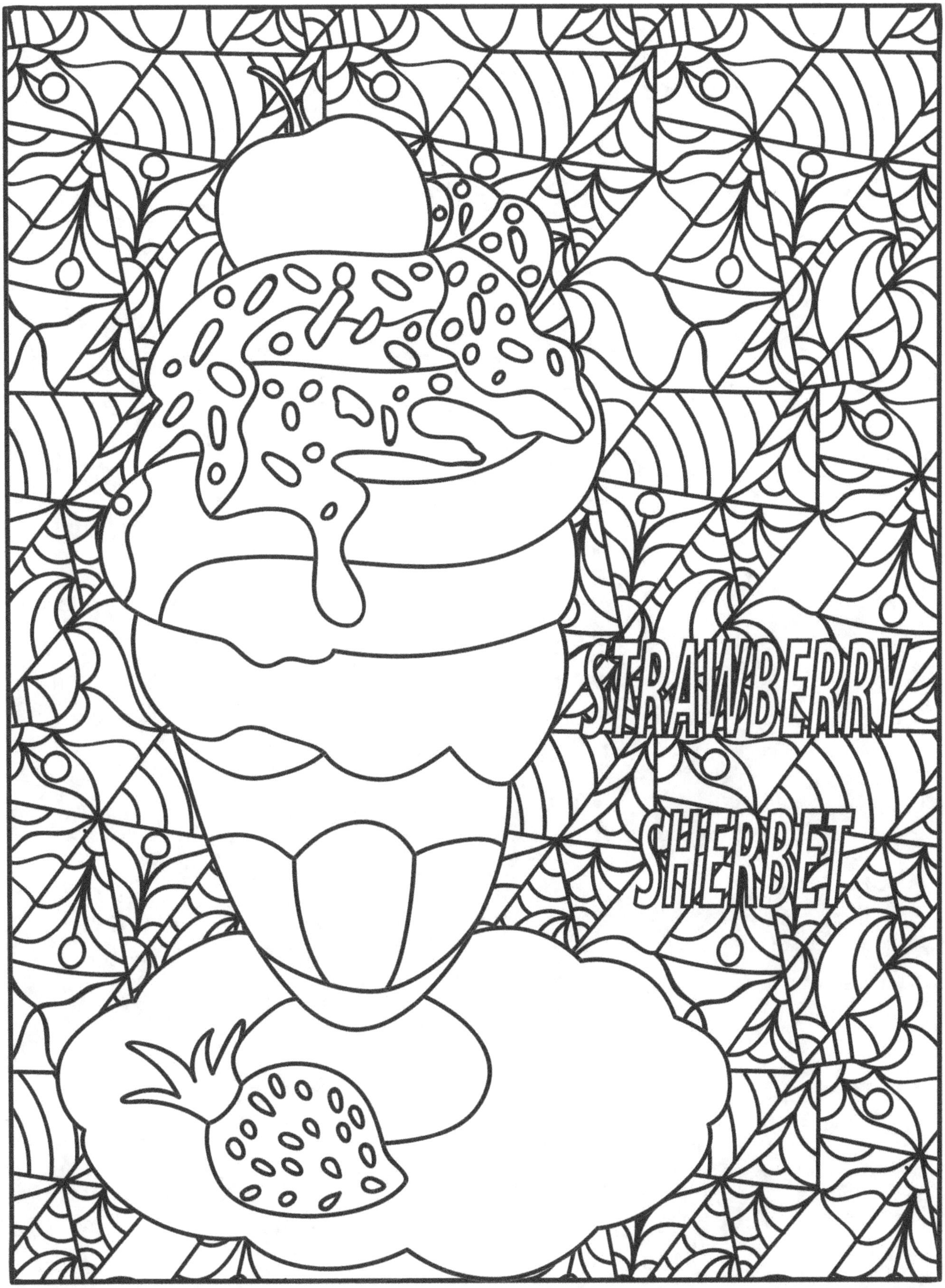
STRAWBERRY
SHERBET

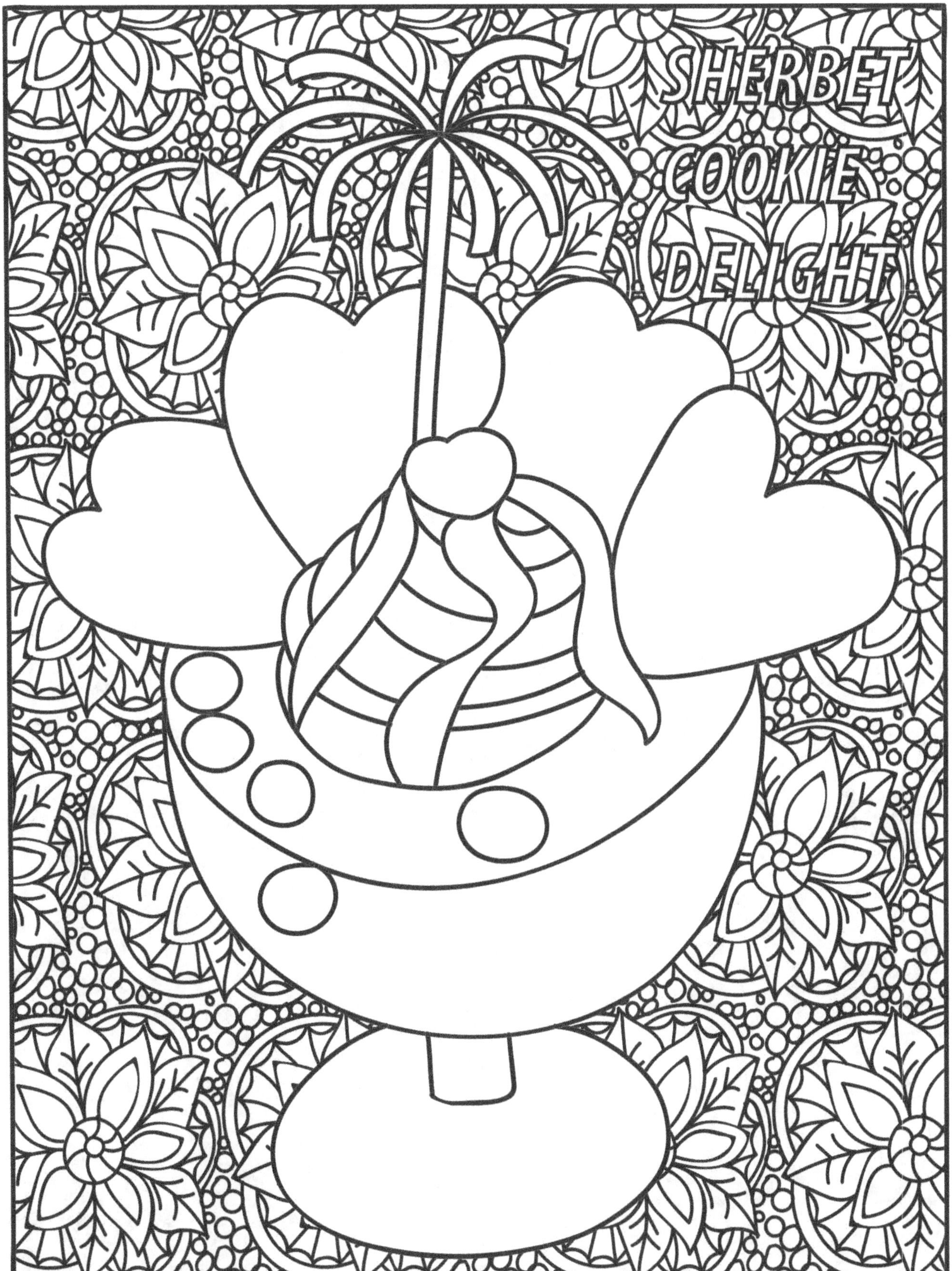
SHERBET
COOKIE
DELIGHT

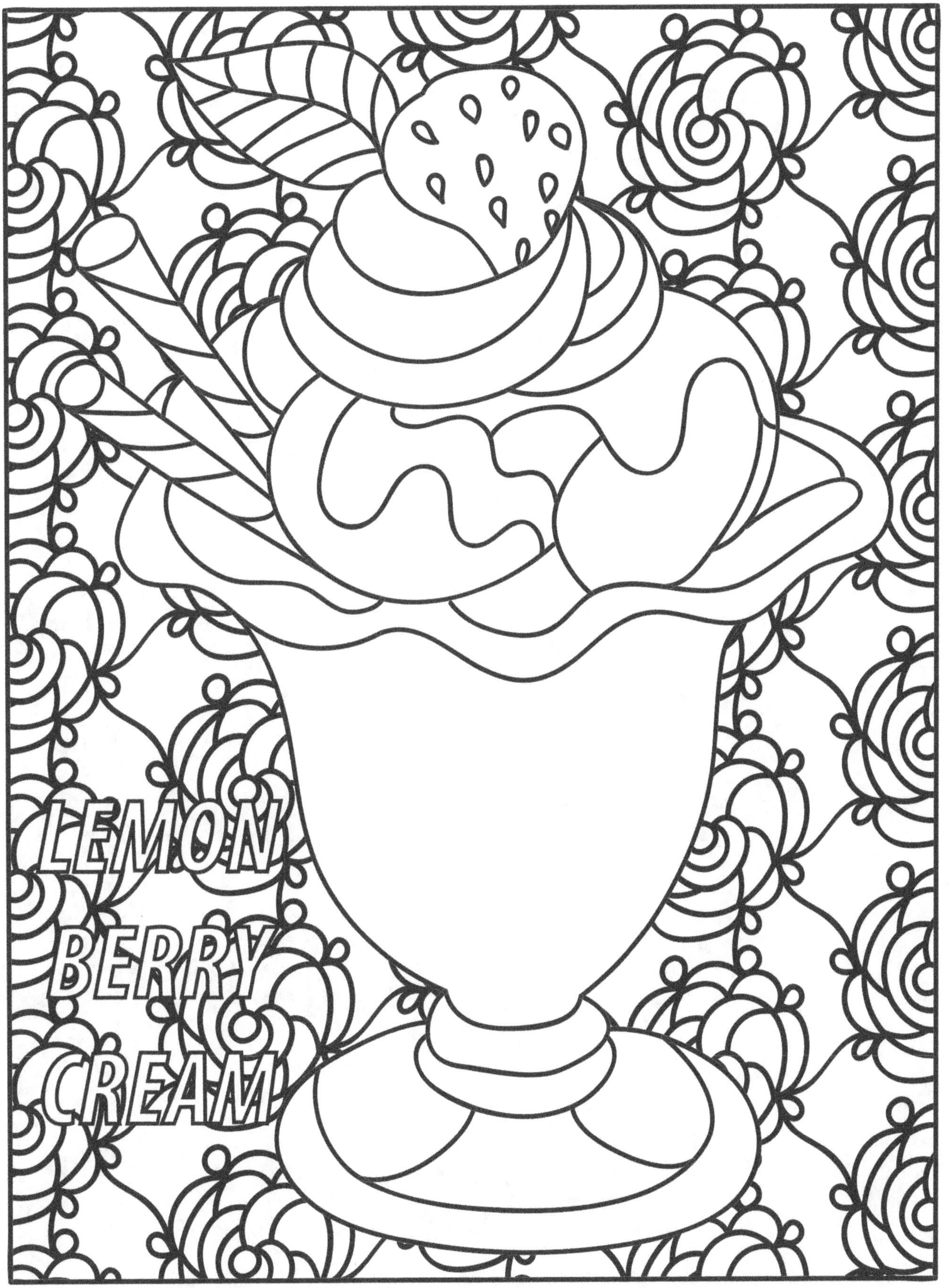
LEMON
BERRY
CREAM

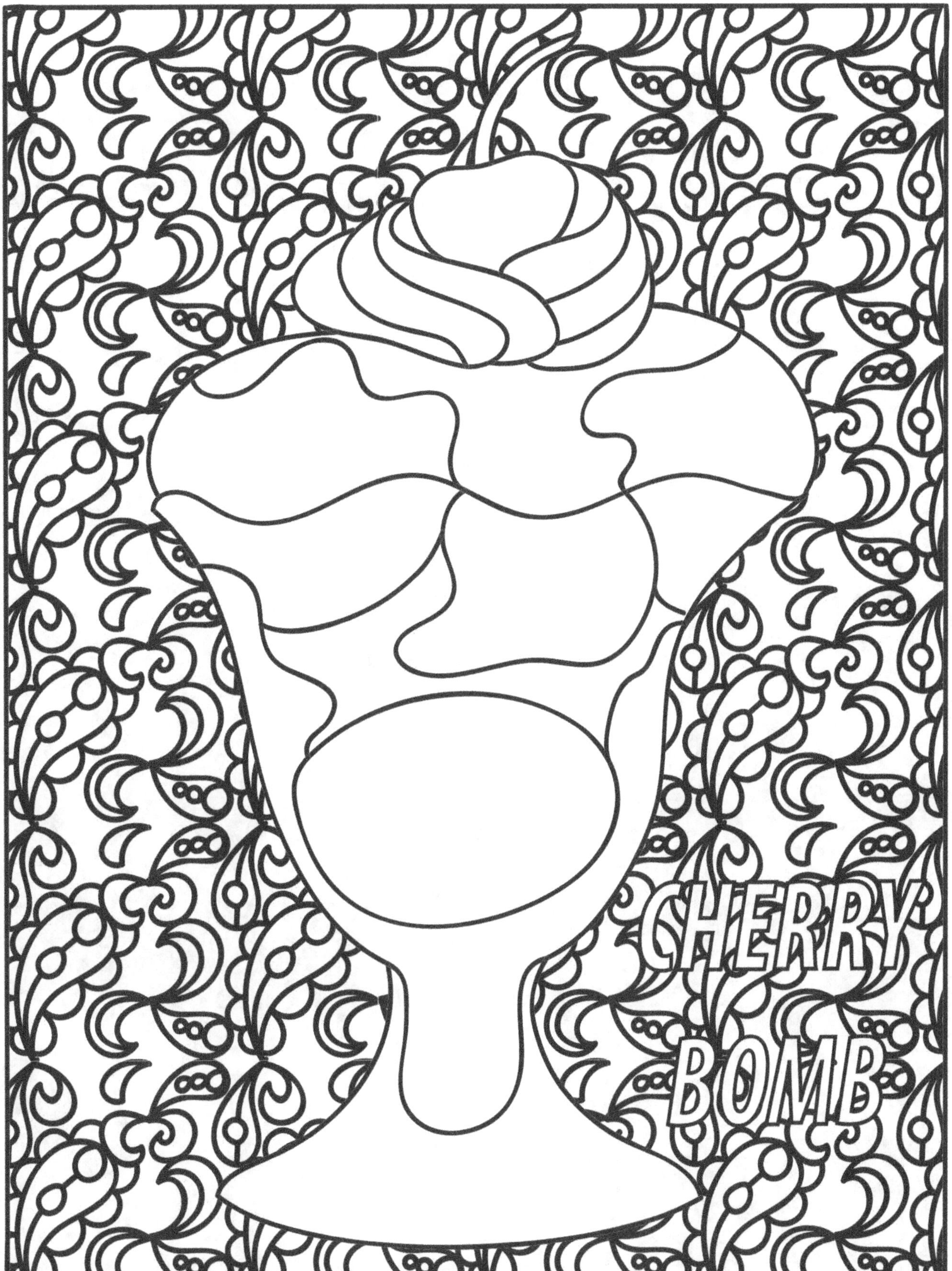
CHERRY
BOMB

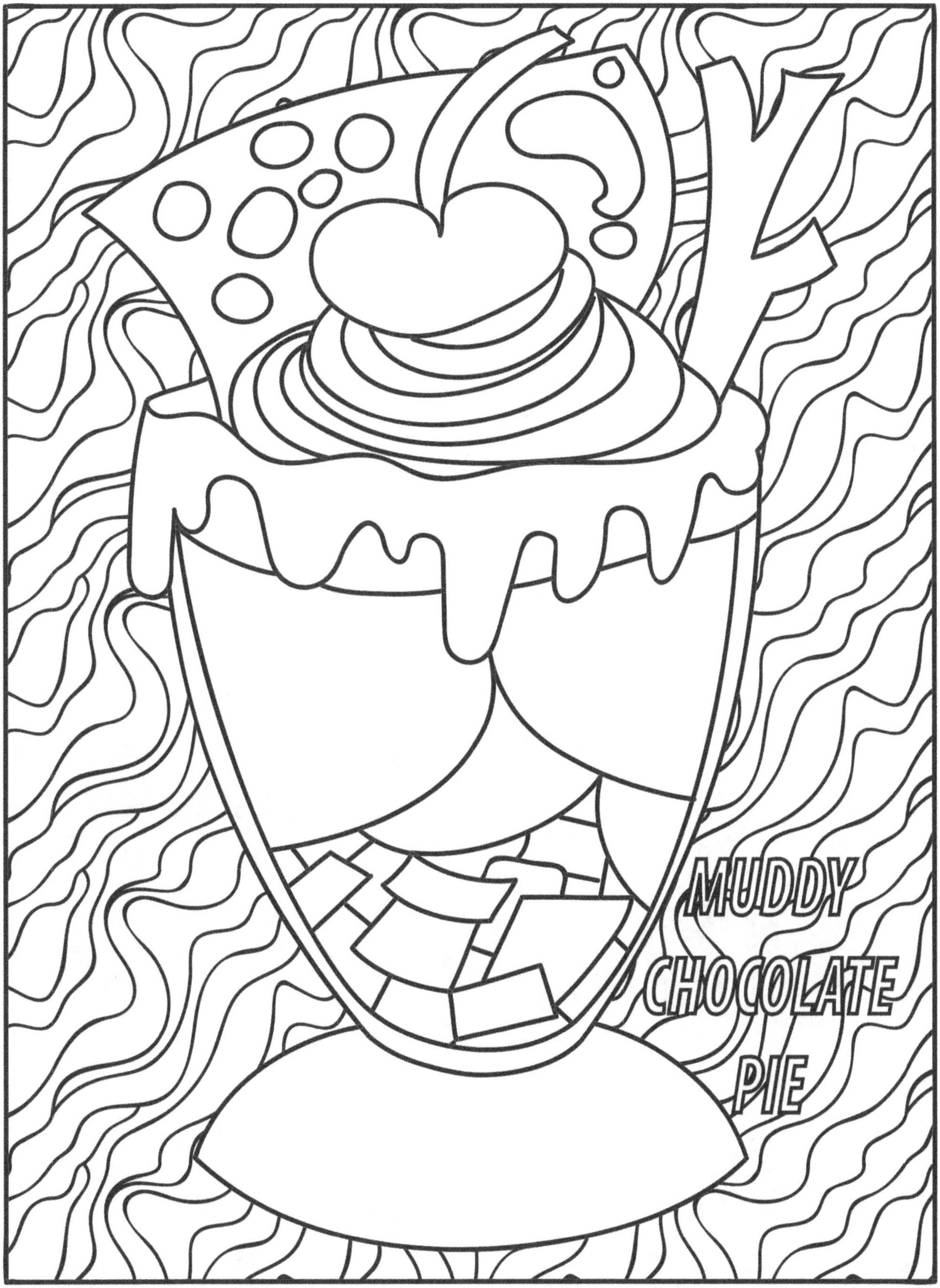
MUDDY
CHOCOLATE
PIE

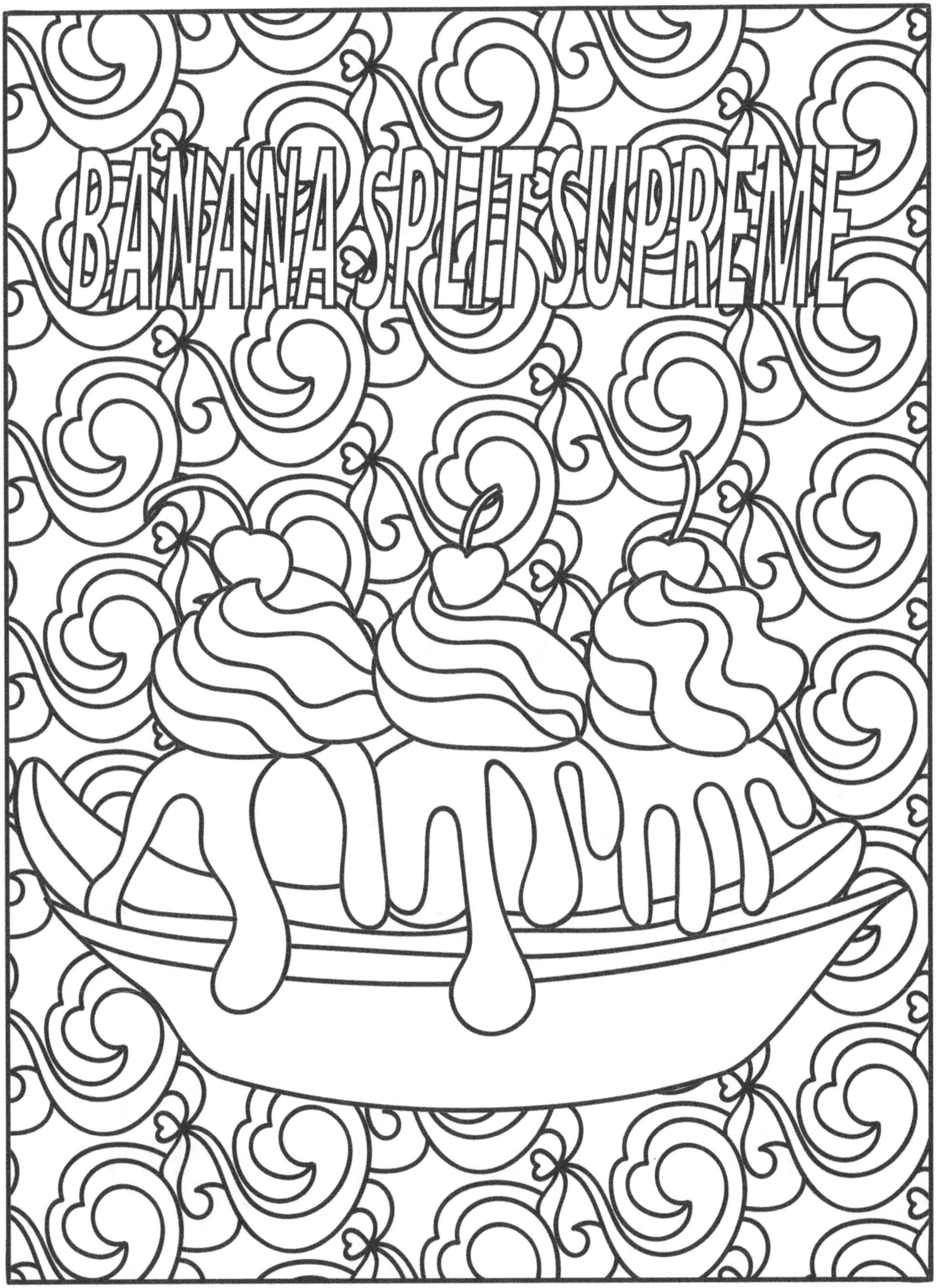
BANANA SPLIT SUPREME

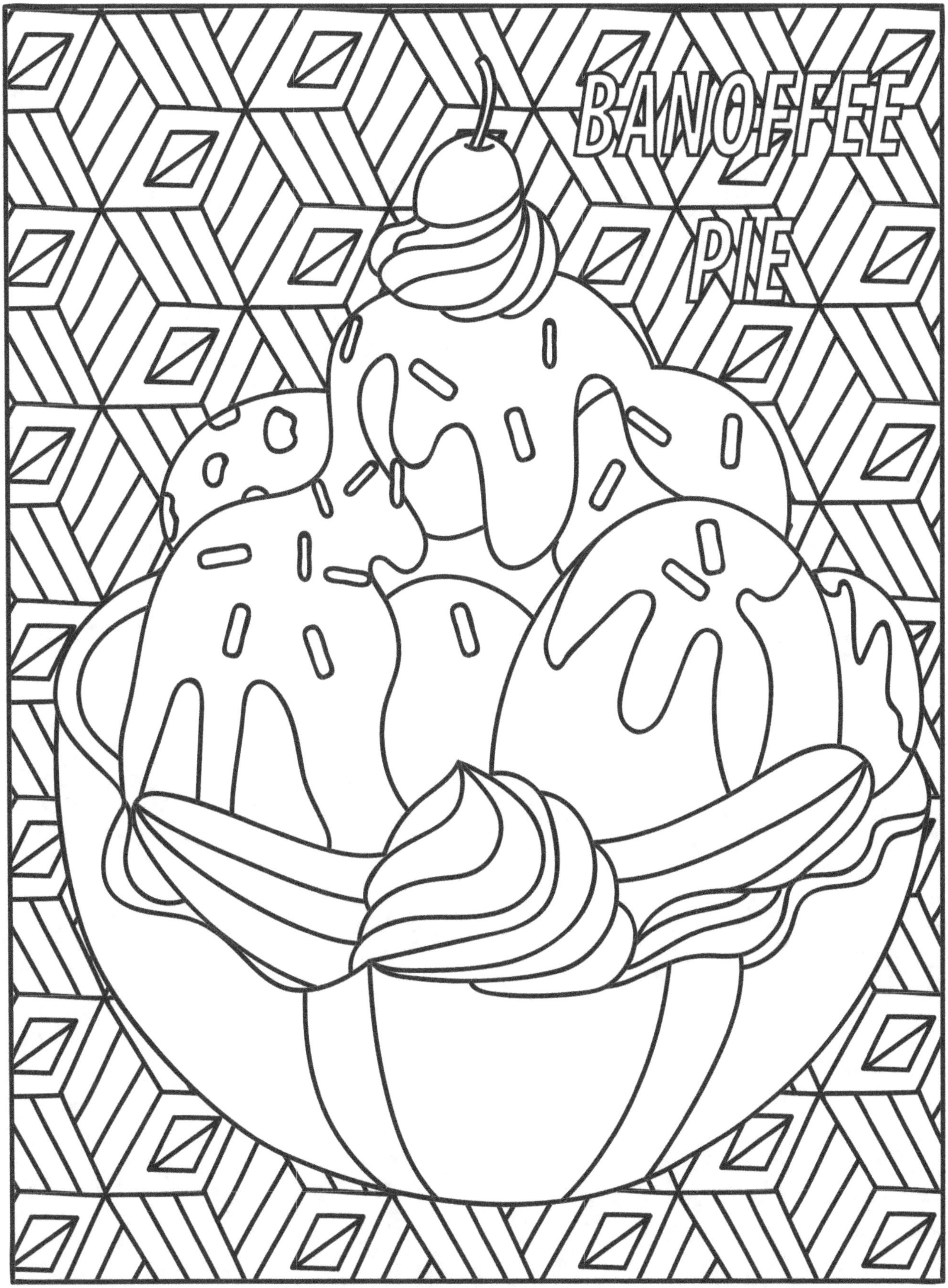
BANOFFEE
PIE

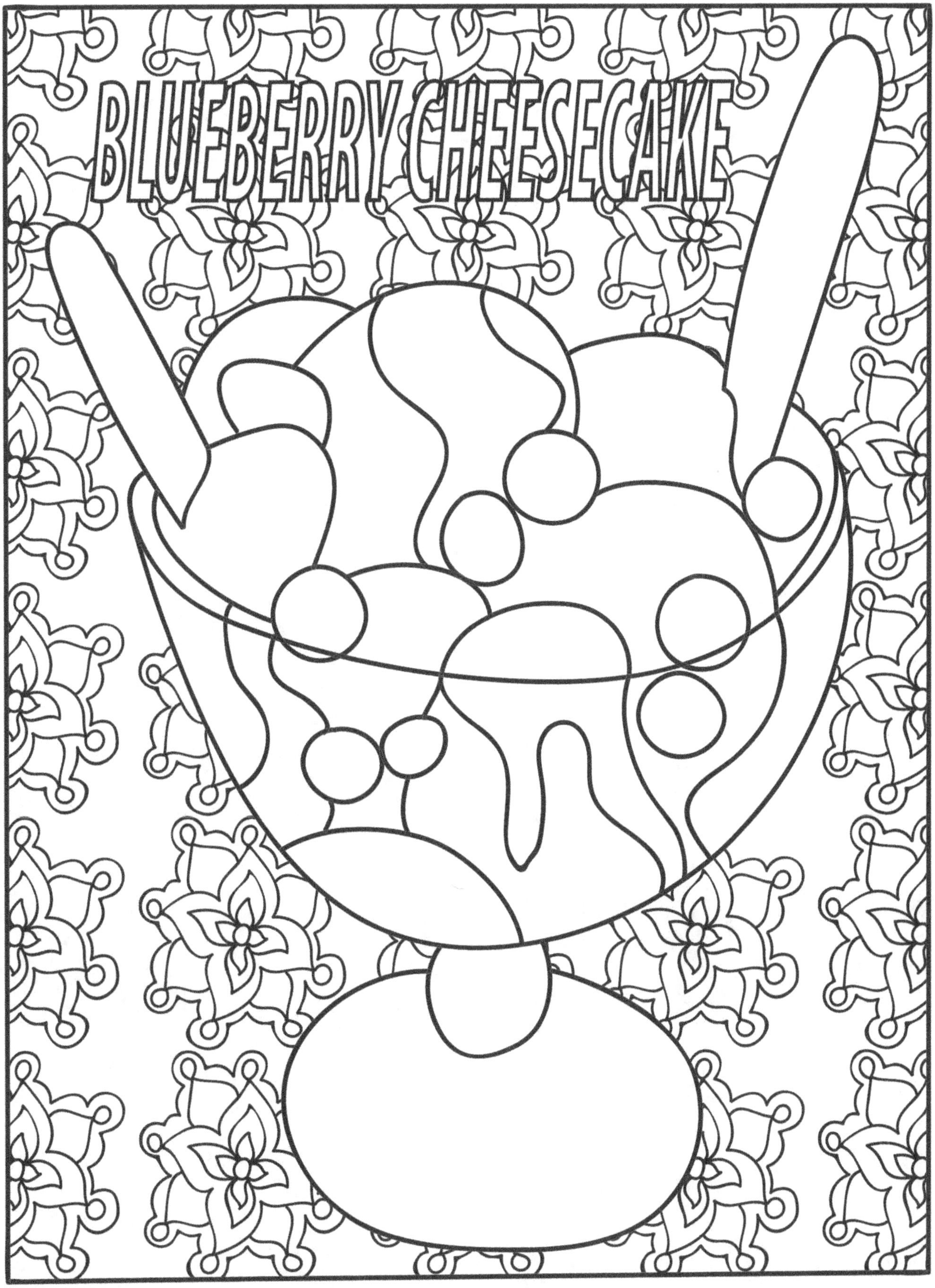
BLUEBERRY CHEESECAKE

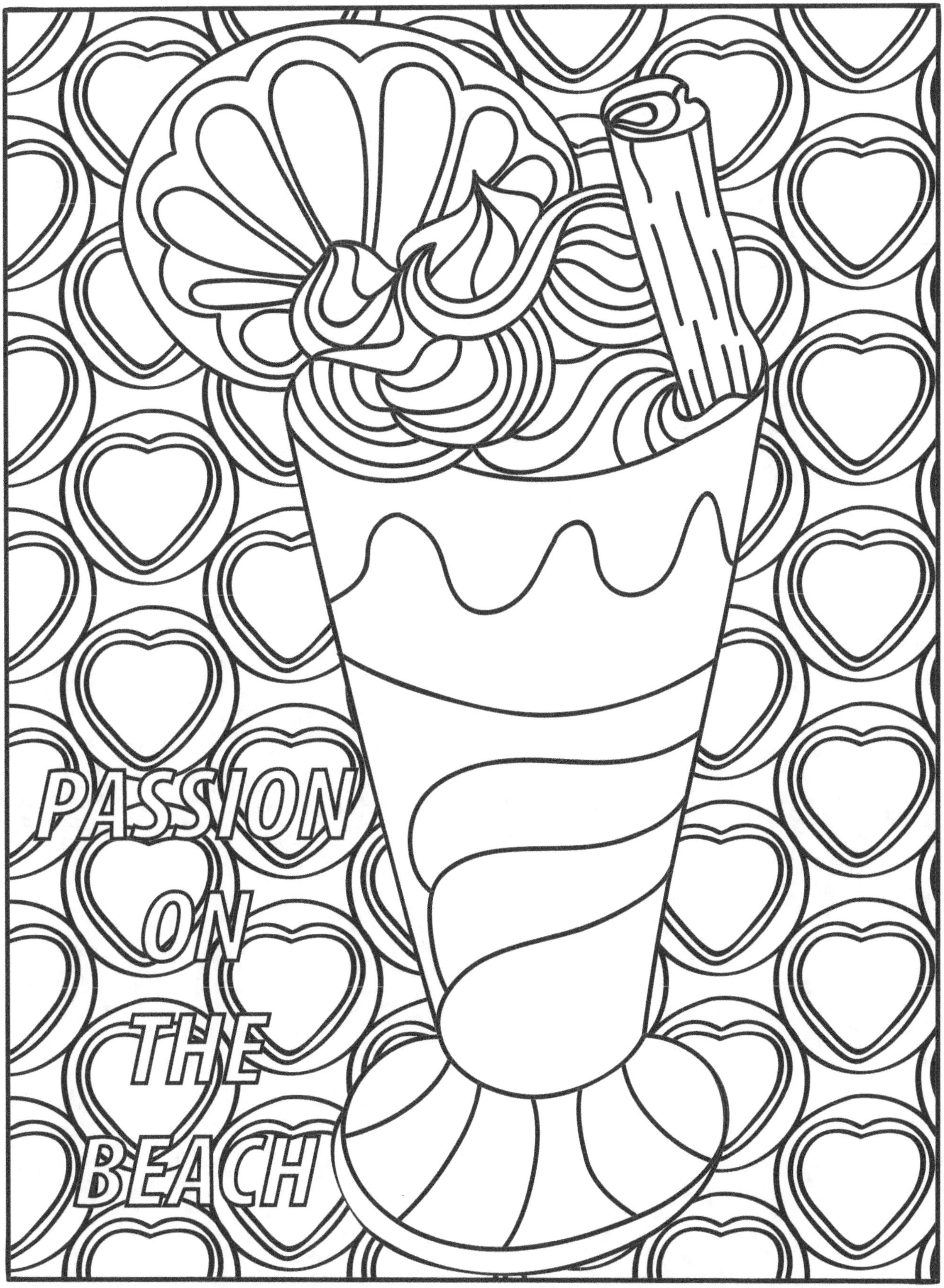
PASSION
ON
THE
BEACH

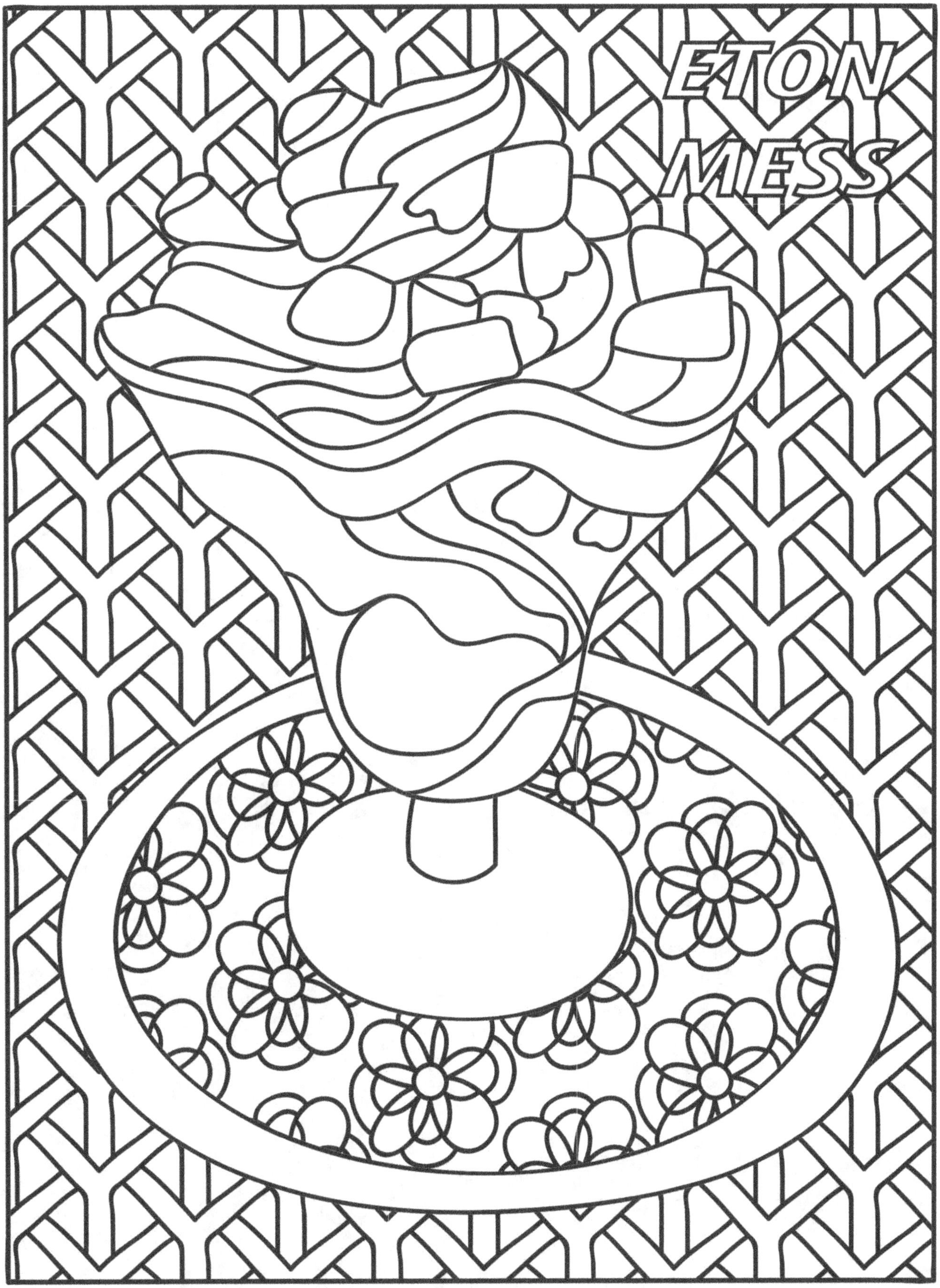
ETON
MESS

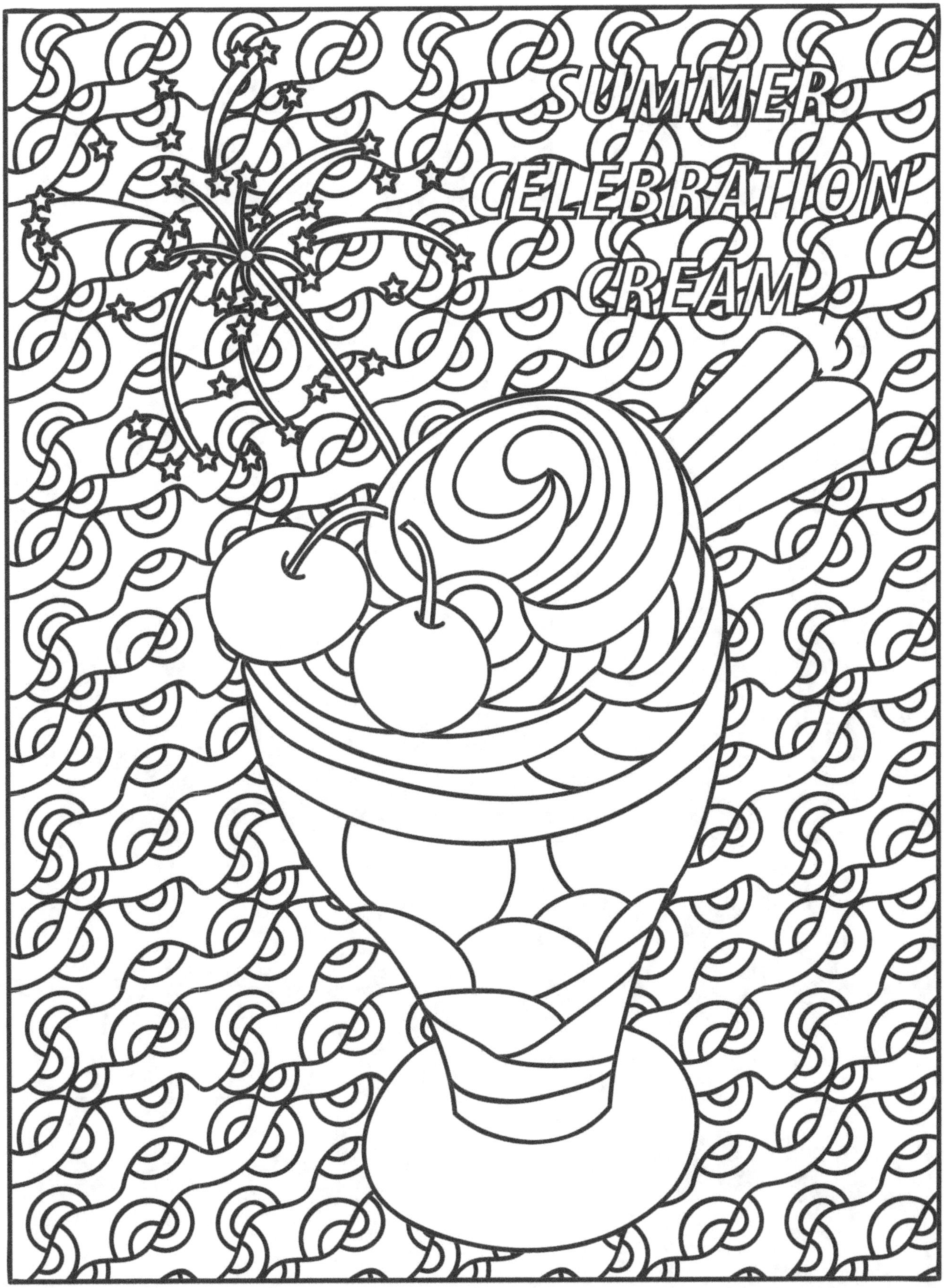
SUMMER
CELEBRATION
CREAM

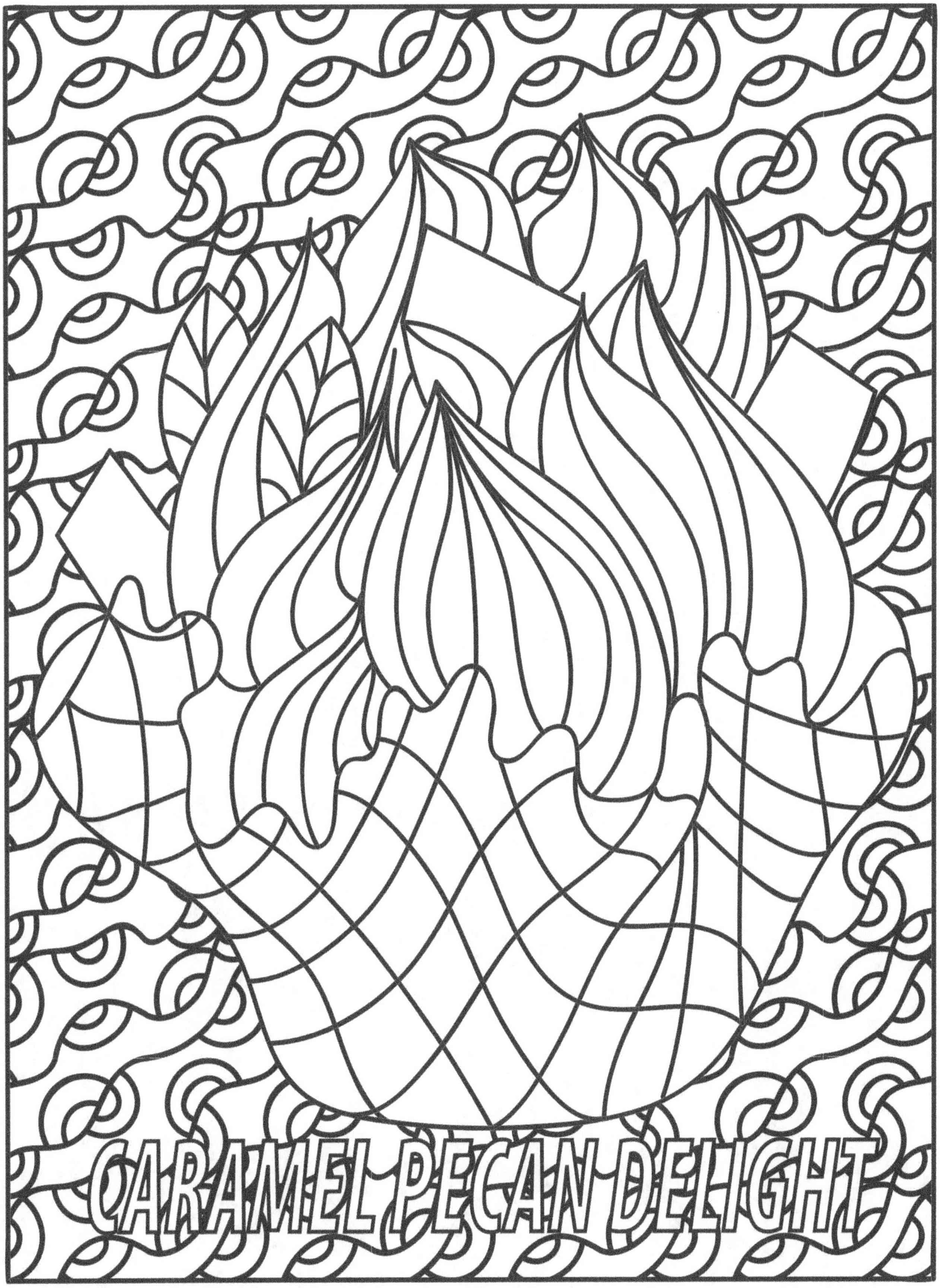
CARAMEL PECAN DELIGHT

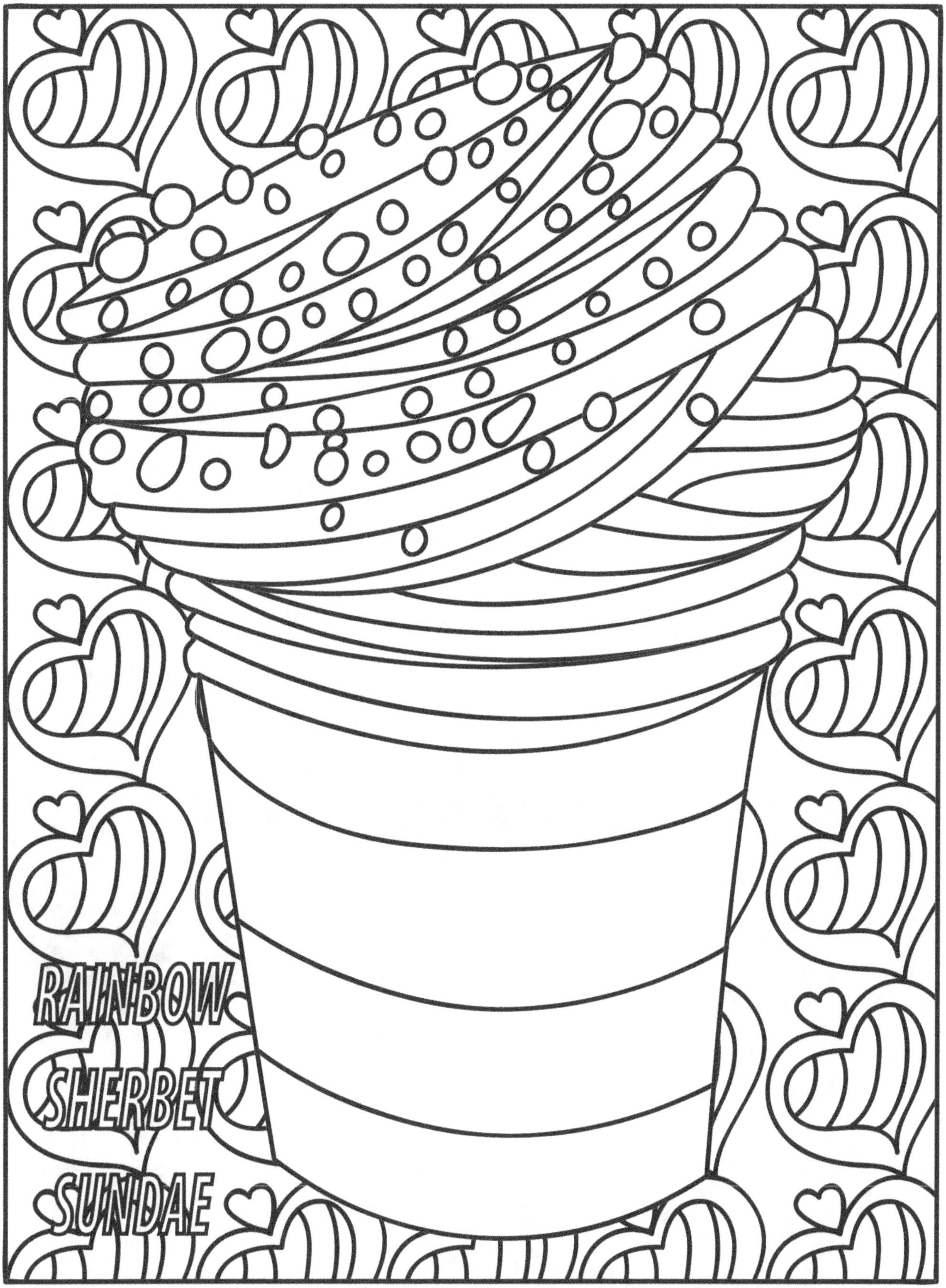
RAINBOW
SHERBET
SUNDAE

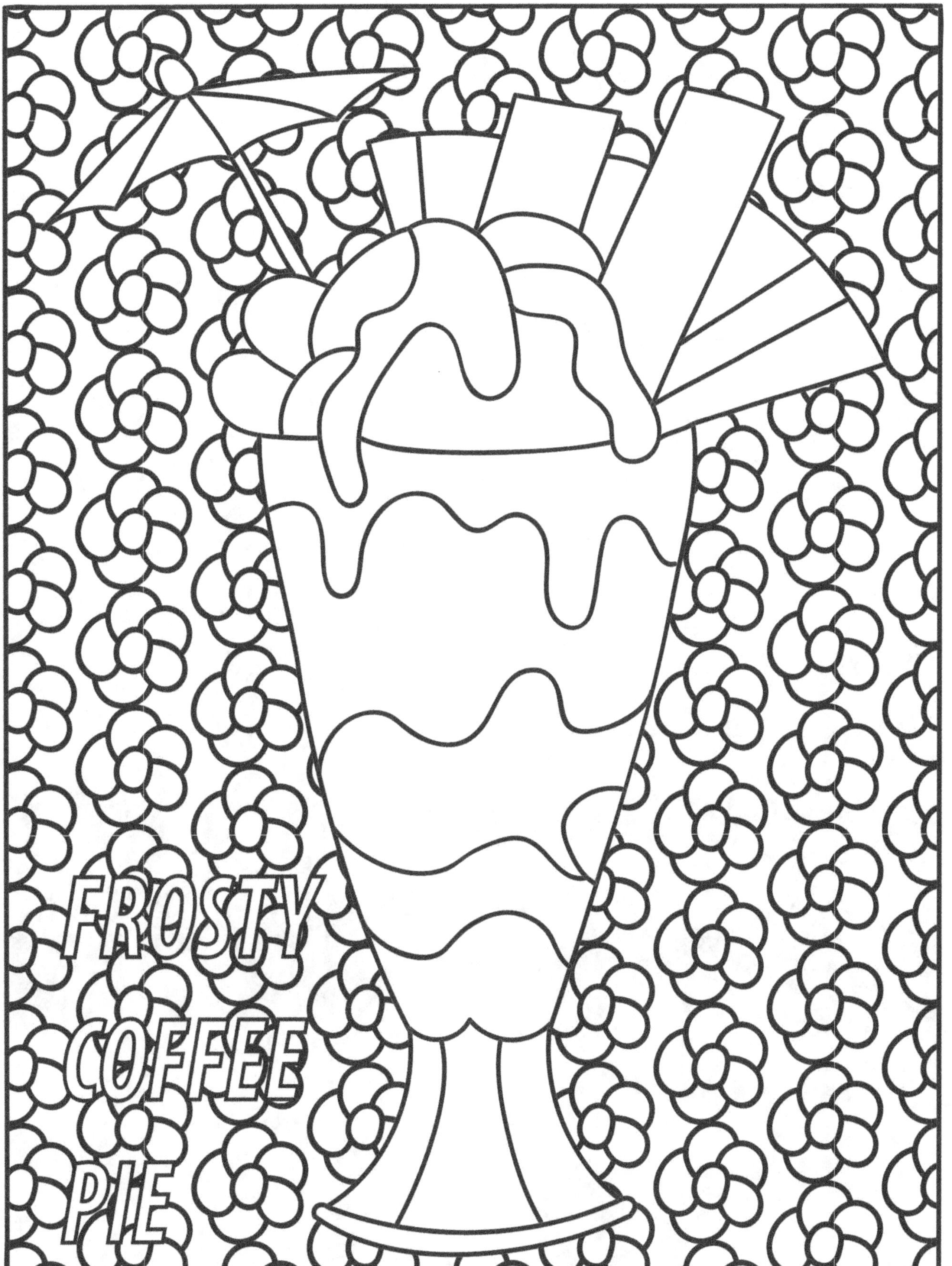
FROSTY
COFFEE
PIE

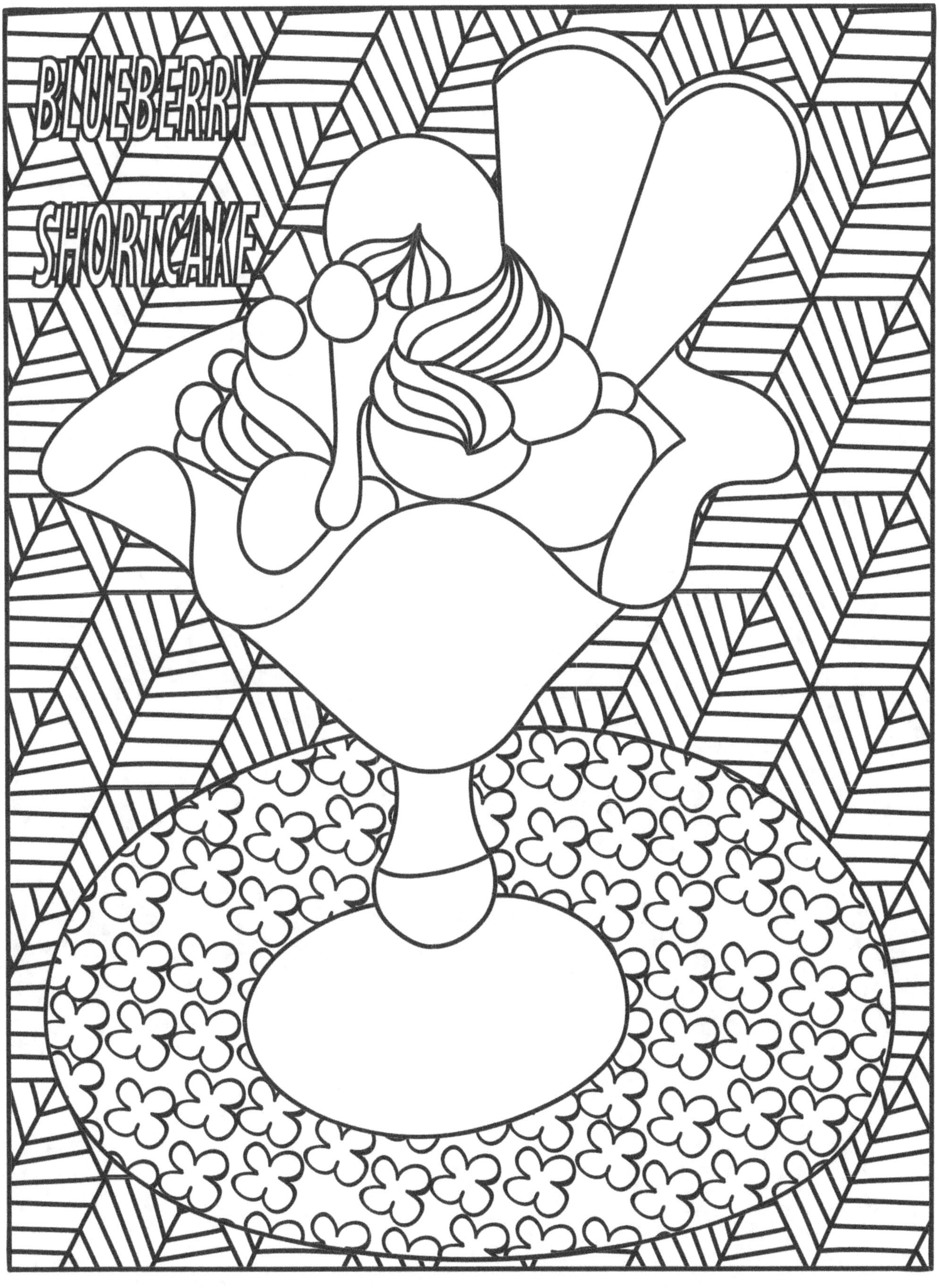
BLUEBERRY
SHORTCAKE

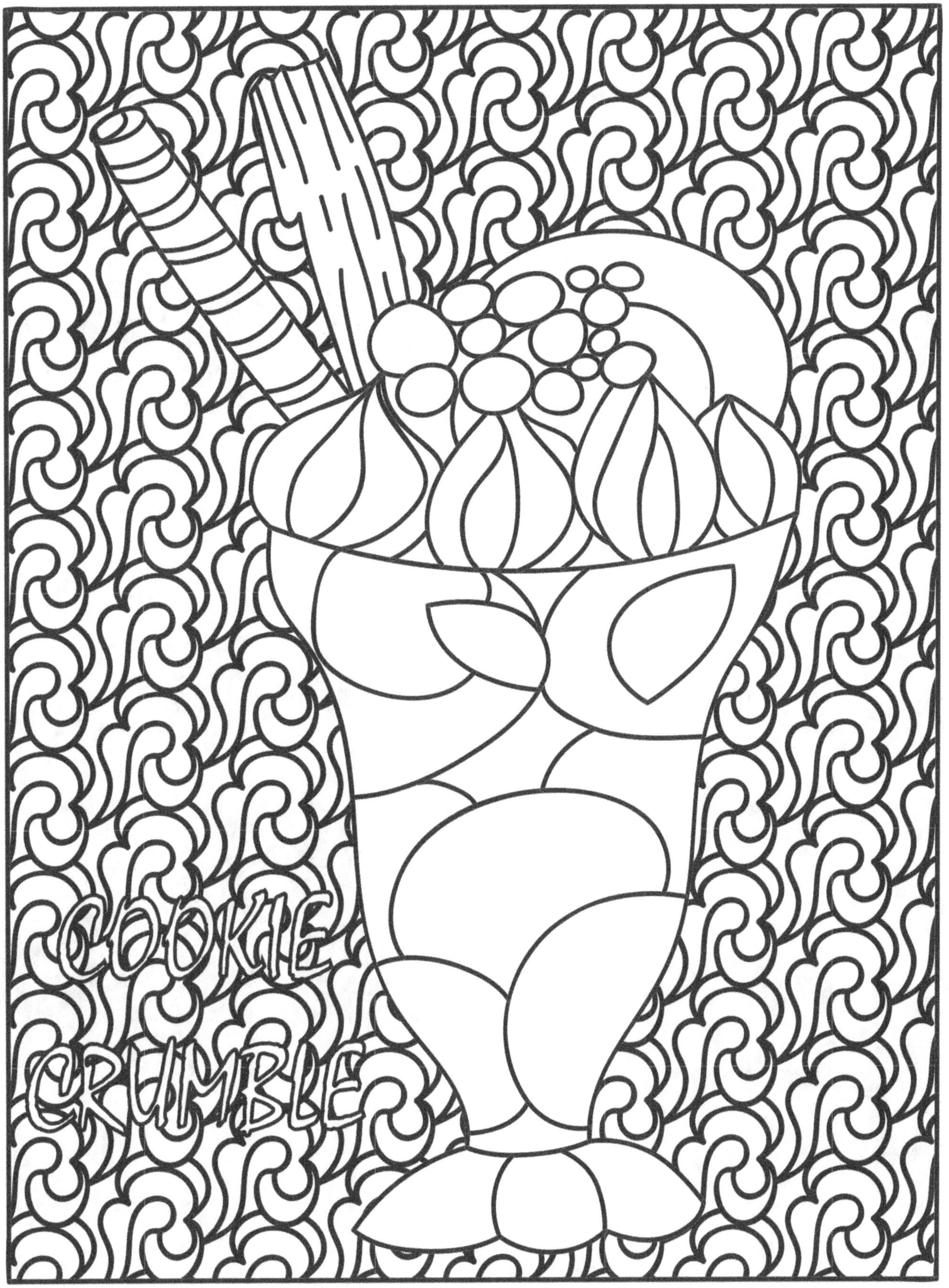
COOKIE
CRUMBLE

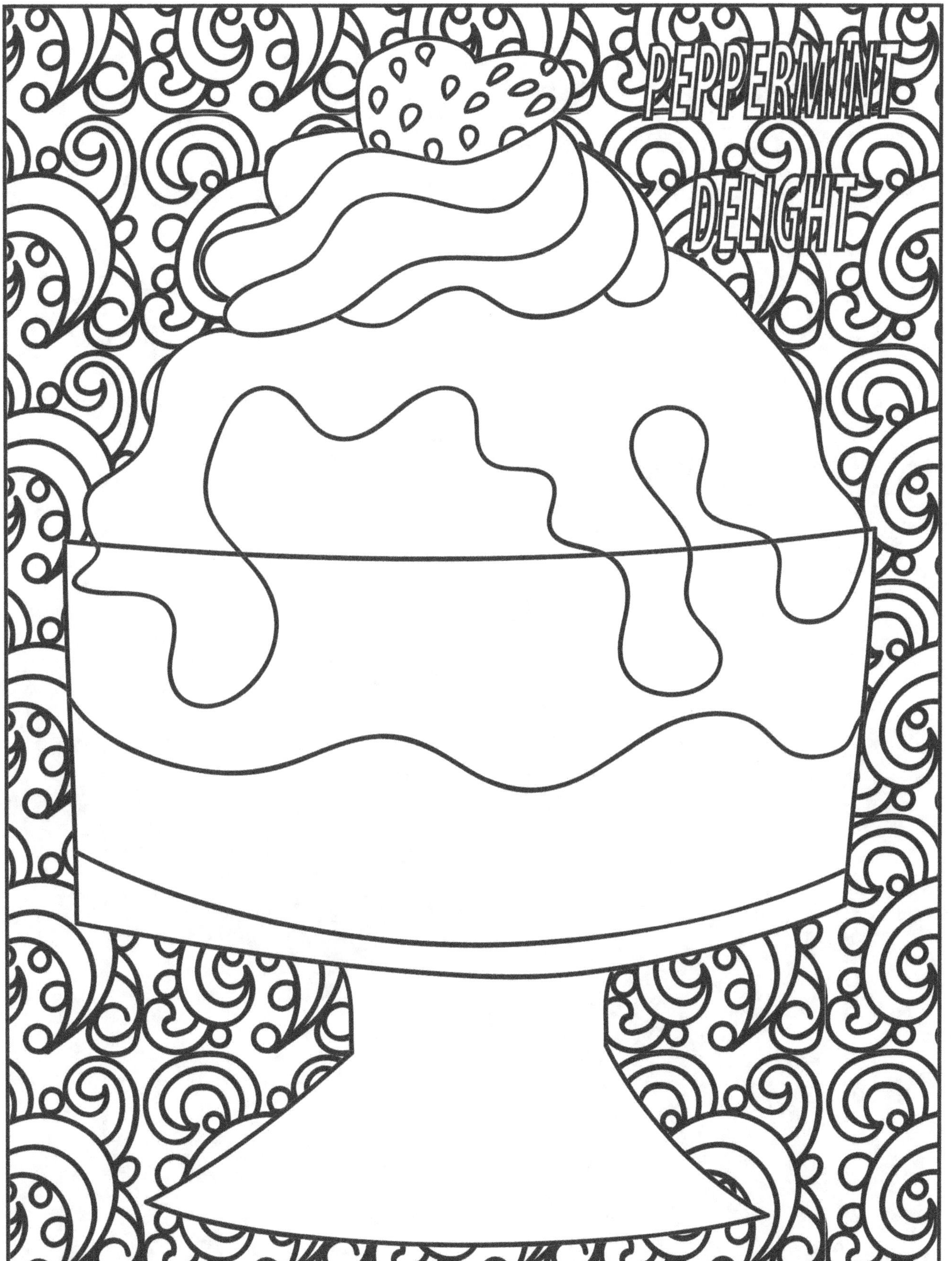
PEPPERMINT
DELIGHT

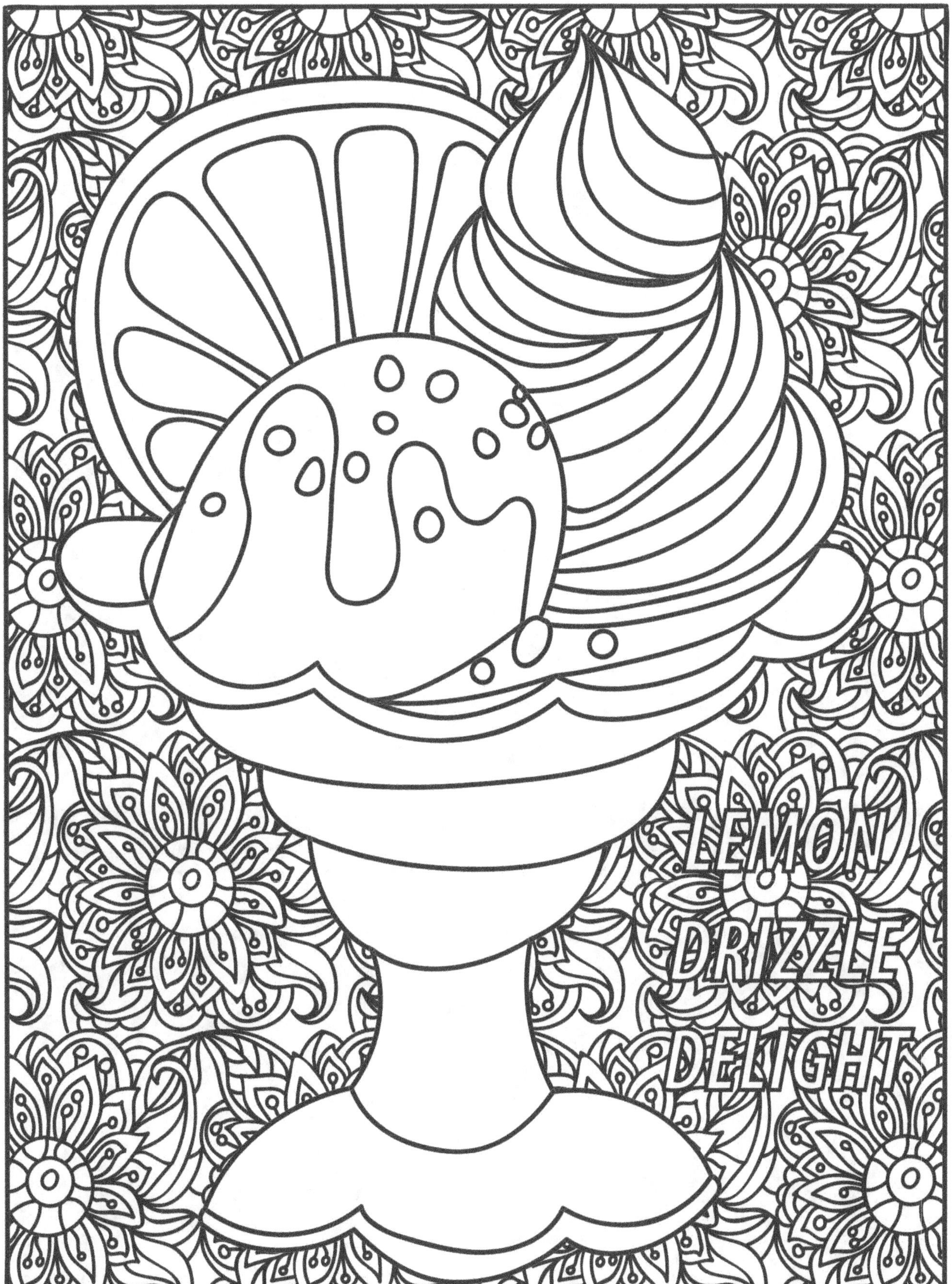
LEMON
DRIZZLE
DELIGHT

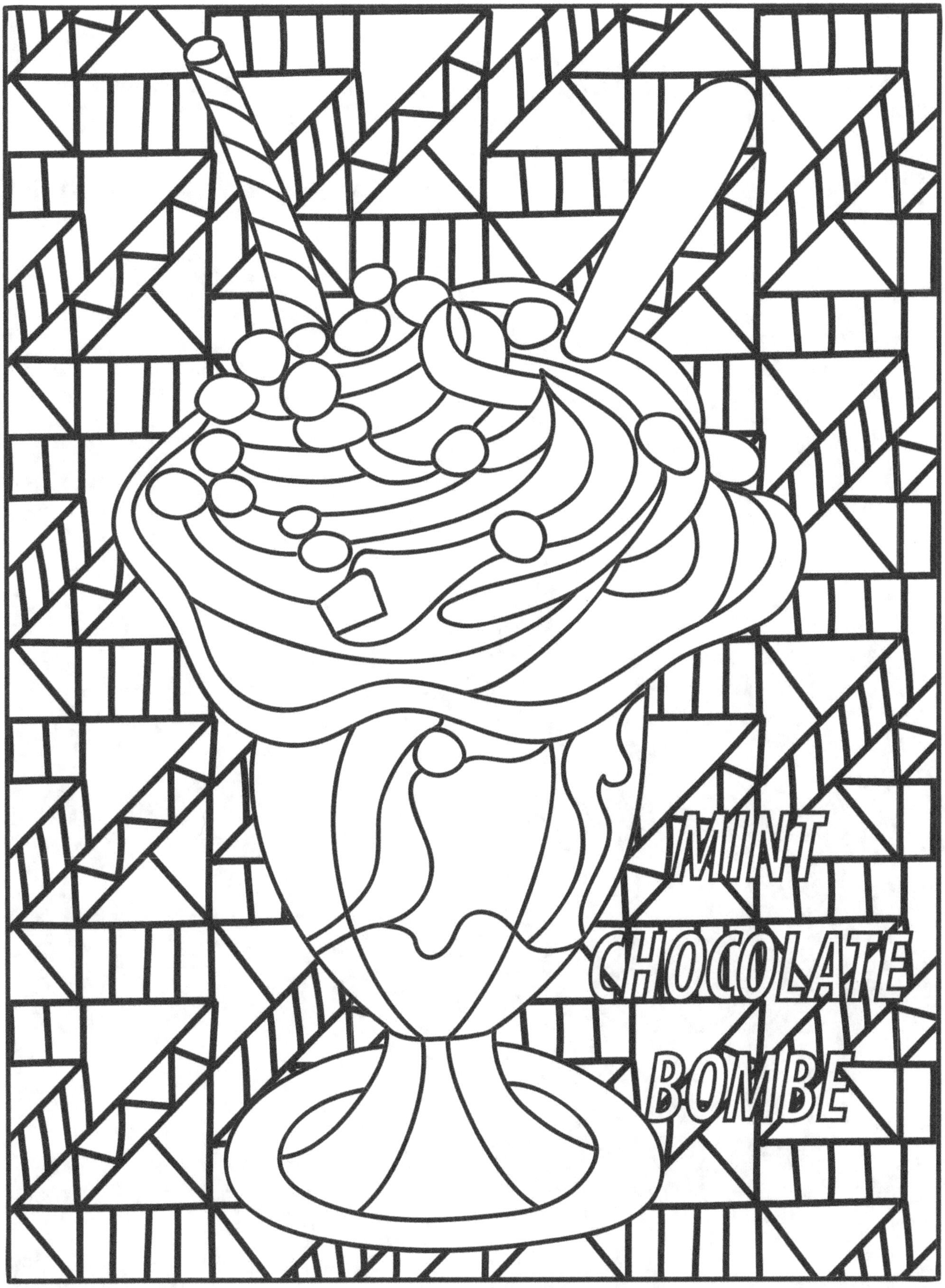
MINT
CHOCOLATE
BOMBE

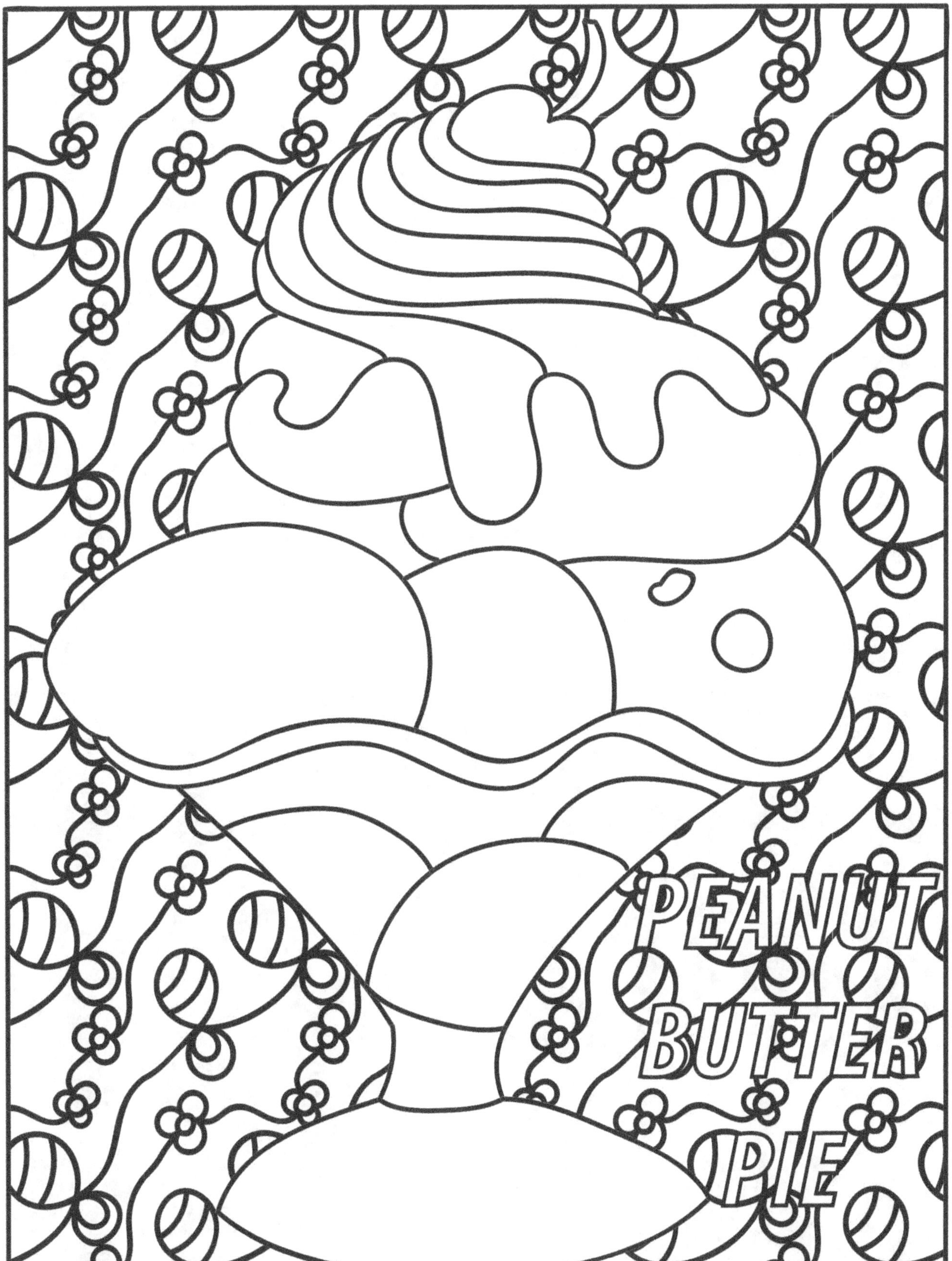
PEANUT
BUTTER
PIE

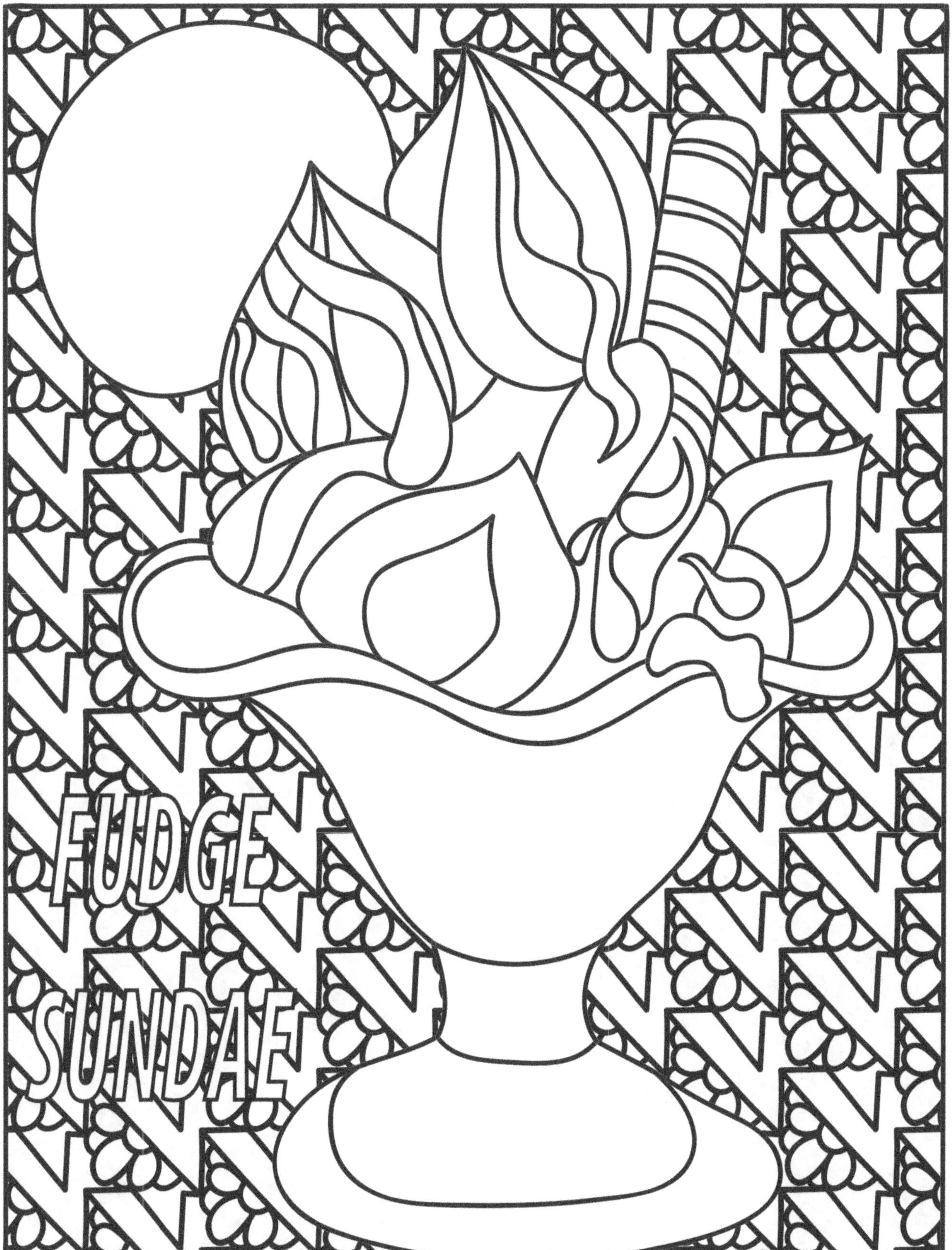
FUDGE
SUNDAE

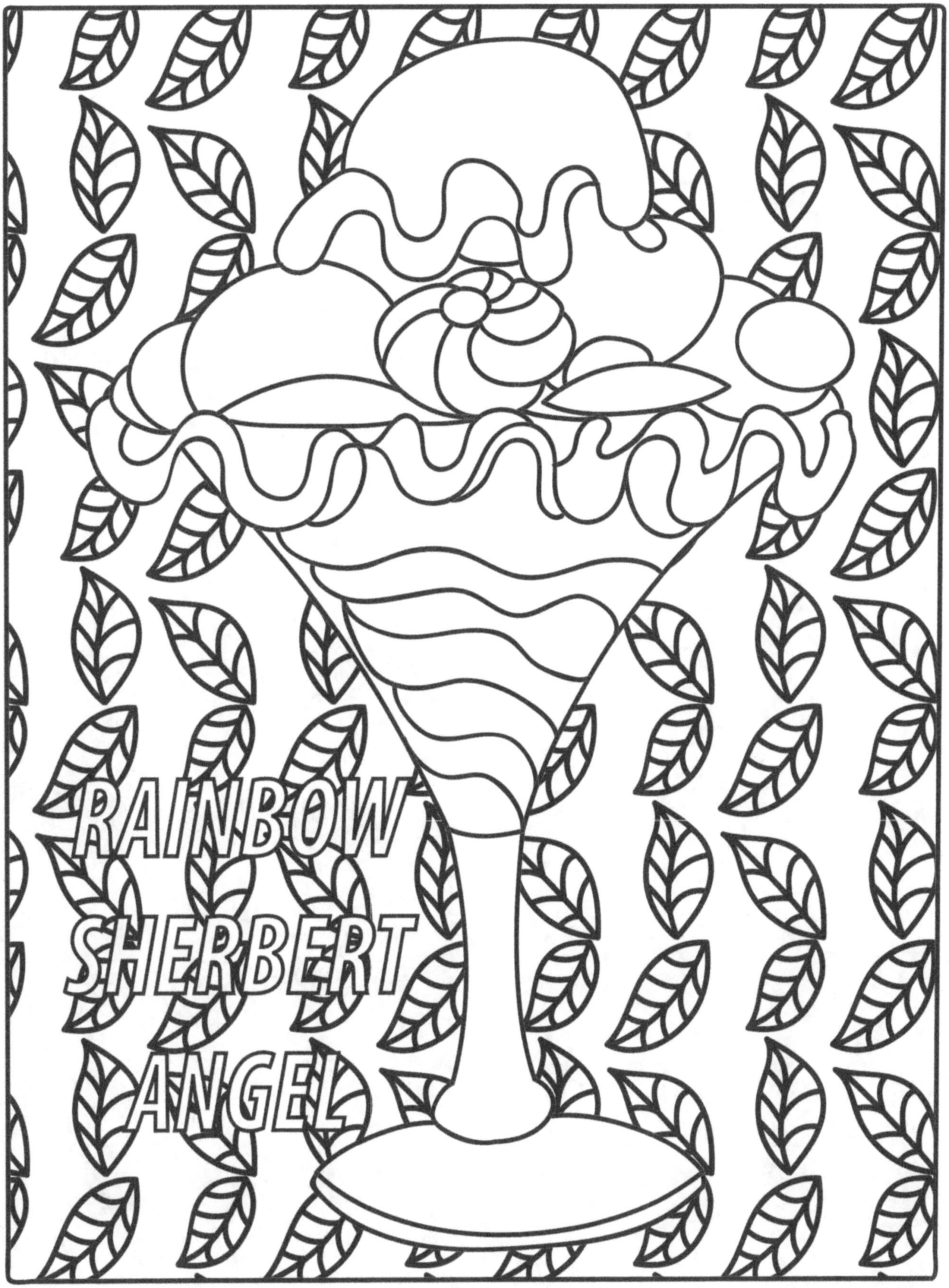
RAINBOW
SHERBERT
ANGEL

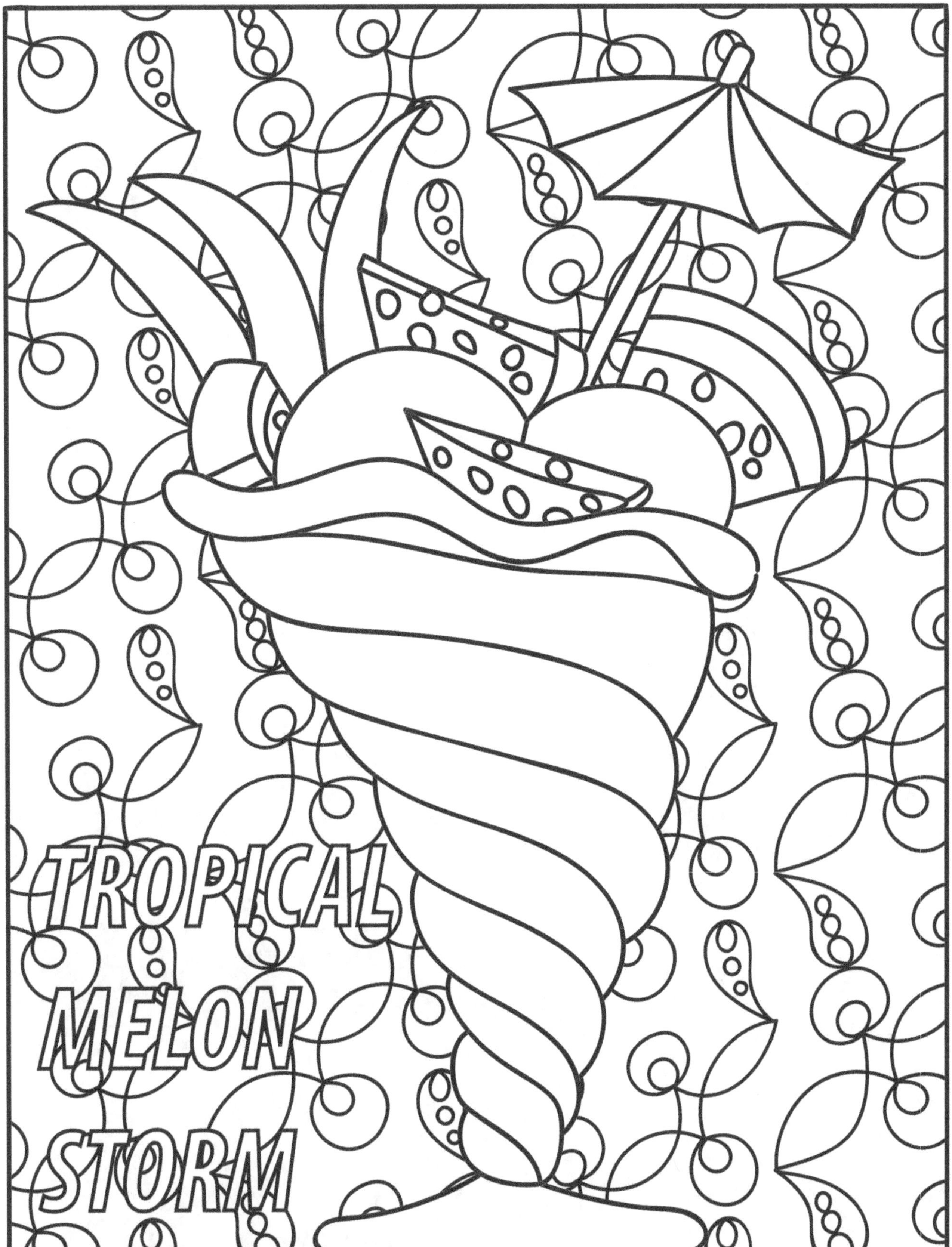
TROPICAL
MELON
STORM

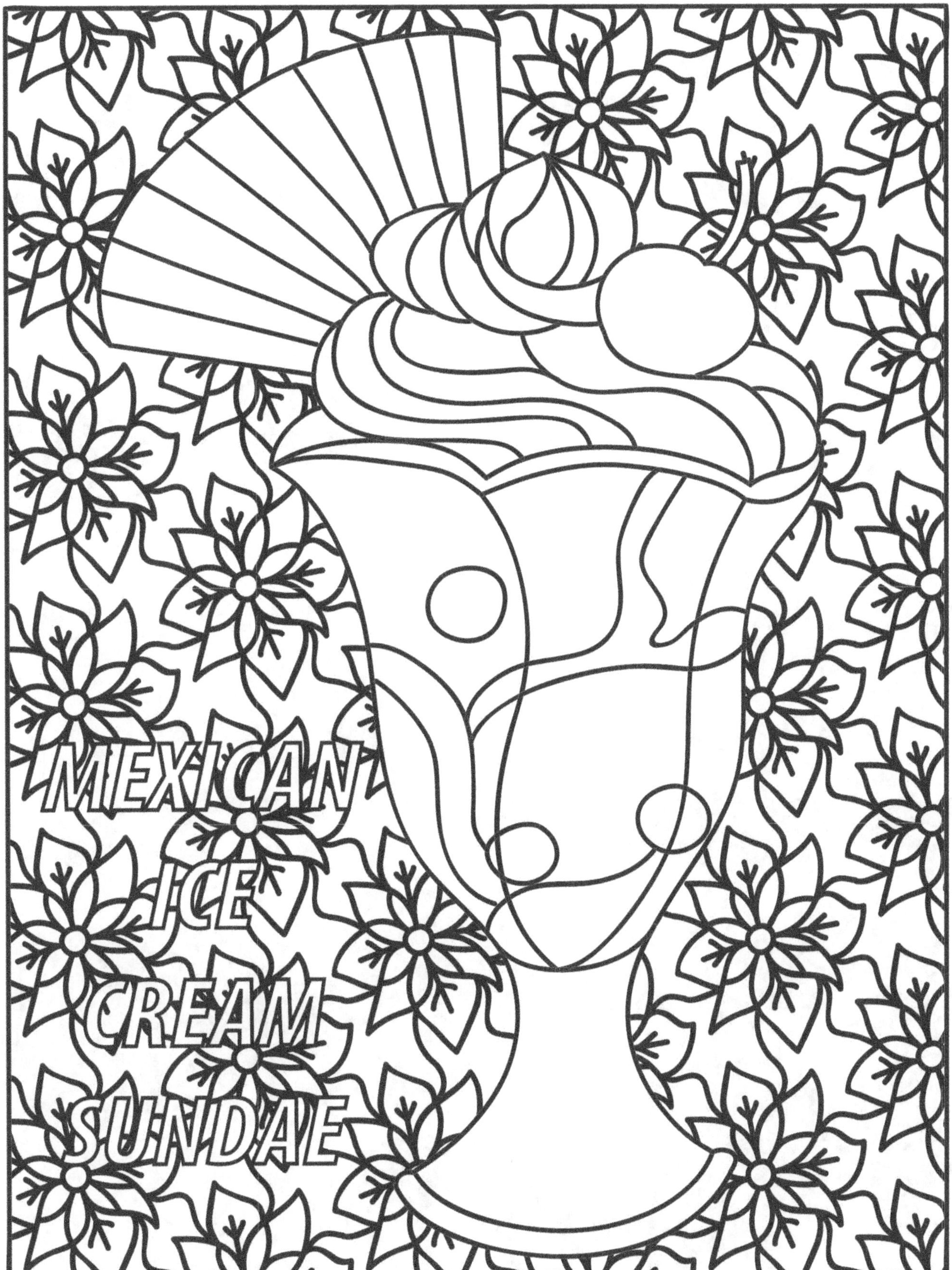
MEXICAN
ICE
CREAM
SUNDAE

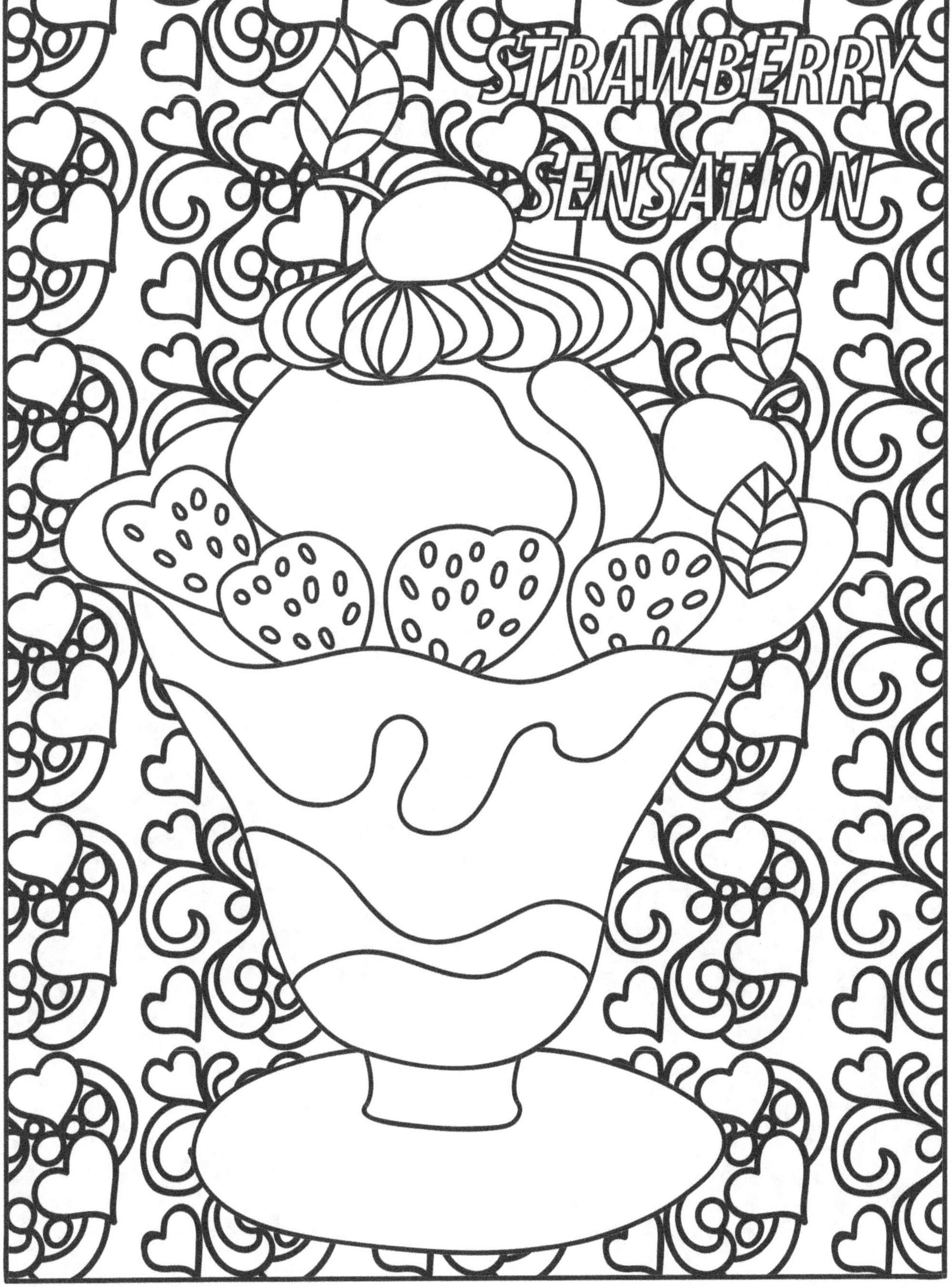
STRAWBERRY
SENSATION

COLOR TEST PAGE

COLOR TEST PAGE

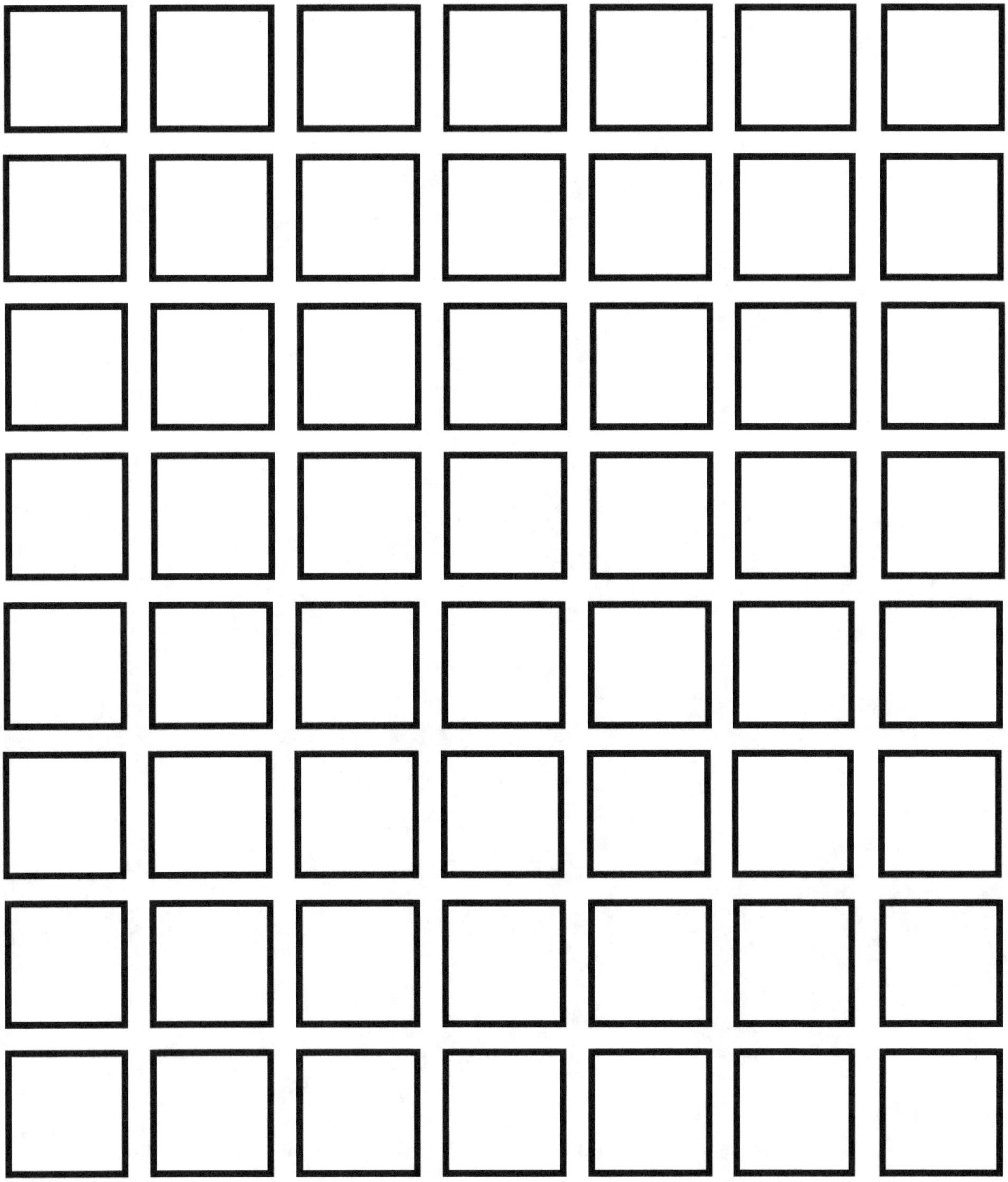

www.ingramcontent.com/pod-product-compliance
Lightning Source LLC
Chambersburg PA
CBHW081016170526
45158CB00010B/3055
* 9 7 8 1 0 9 0 7 4 3 0 0 8 *